A Gran Scheme

Other books By Shelley Beer

Un Lucky!

A La Carte for the Mind

Violation of Beauty

Revenge Maid Easy

And a collection of children's "tails" for the little ones!

A Rose for Violet, Mischievous Rose

Floral Tails, Pawprint Moments

A Gran Scheme

Shelley Beer

*I'm hoping this book is the apple of your eye!
Warm wishes,
Shelley*

This book is a work of fiction. Names, characters, places and incidents are the products of the author's imagination or are used fictitiously. Any resemblance to places, actual events or persons living or dead is purely coincidental.

Copyright © 2025 by Shelley Beer

All rights reserved. No part of this book may be reproduced in any form or by any electronic or mechanical means including information storage and retrieval systems – except in the case of brief quotations embodied in critical articles or reviews – without permission in writing from its author.

No part of this book may be used or reproduced in any way for the purpose of training artificial intelligence technologies or systems.

This book was written in its entirety by Shelley Beer and no AI was used in the process.

To all those I adore, remember you will always be loved unconditionally and be treasured forever in my heart. Never forget the importance of grandparents, they are sacred in the minds of grandchildren. Offering an endless supply of love and patience, they always have open arms. And that's the key to a very special relationship.

A Gran Scheme

Chapter 1

Dr. Chloe Burke sat in her office at the French antique desk with its bronze accents gazing at the locket that graced her neck everyday. It was 18k gold, oval in shape and set with diamonds on the outside, but it was the inside that she treasured the most. It embraced three very sentimental photographs. The first one was of her mother, Arabella Burke boasting her contagious smile that could light up not just a room, but a whole city. The bright red lipstick contrasted against her porcelain skin complementing the golden chestnut hair that framed her face and warm hazel eyes. Her mother was also an optometrist like herself and that was the true reason that she had chosen the profession, to honor her memory. This had once been her clinic which she ran with her associate Dr. Neil Benson and Chloe didn't have it in her heart to change a single thing. The quaint two storey building was happily wedged between a law office and a high-end ladies' shop in the heart of downtown Oakville. Boston ivy clung to a small section of the front and side brick reaching the roofline of the second storey. A French balcony with intricate wrought iron above the glossy black door was home to a large window box filled with hot pink geraniums in the summer. It held a selection of evergreen branches and pine combs throughout the winter months complete with an enormous bow. The sign which matched the door, bore the name *Royal Eye Care* in beautiful gilt.

Her mother had found the stunning desk while antiquing with her father many years ago and purchased it for the office along with the chair. After completing her Bachelor of Science degree with Honours, Chloe continued at the University of Waterloo obtaining a Doctor of Optometry degree. The internship continued with Dr. Neil Benson, or Doc Benson as everyone called him with Chloe becoming his associate just before her 26th birthday. He was a special soul, with a depth to his personality like no other. Considerate to a fault, he groomed her into a skilled and empathetic doctor to which she would forever be indebted. Glenda, now 62 years young was the original receptionist when her mother first started at the optometrist office with Doc Benson years ago. She was a real blessing to have. Everything in the office whispered her mother's touch, from the furnishings to the artwork on the wall. Even the bronze textured wallpaper sang her praises. Born Arabella Dawson, she married Chloe's father Grayson Burke when she was twenty-four years old. Tears welled up in Chloe's eyes as she looked at the next photograph of her father, running her fingers gently over his face. He was ruggedly handsome with blue eyes, dark blonde hair and a well manicured beard. He also had a heart of gold. A well-loved veterinarian who never charged anyone if they couldn't afford to pay and reduced the bill for those who could pay just a little. Mother always teased that good thing she was earning well, or they would have starved. But she truly understood his compassion and held the same in her heart. His patients loved their precious pets and so did he. Her daddy had the best sense of humor, always joking about one thing or another and many said that he should be a comedian in his next life. They met when Arabella brought her cat Tabitha, a ginger-colored kitten with vibrant green eyes for a checkup at his clinic. It was an instant connection so it was told, with both blushing and giggling when they spoke to each other. Before she left, he asked her out on a date and it sent her over the moon because she had felt the same way about him. Pretty much until the end, *almost*. She pinched her eyes shut sending the warm, salty tears sliding down her cheeks before reaching blindly for tissue from the box on the desk. Blotting her eyes so she didn't mess up the light makeup that she wore and then blowing her nose, she squeezed it into a ball. She dropped the tissue into the small waste basket by her desk. Chloe sighed and gently closed the locket when the sound of a car pulling into the parking lot reminded her that the next patient had arrived. It was the last appointment of the day and she was exhausted. Peering out of the large bay window, she saw Stanley and his daughter walking slowly up the old cobblestone sidewalk to the front entrance together. He was almost 82 years old and used a walker that she helped him with. Stanley had been her mother's patient for many years before. She opened her office door to greet him as did Glenda and then welcomed him and his daughter into the examination room.

"Stanley, it's so nice to see you. How have you been?" He smiled warmly at her and winked humorously at the receptionist as he pushed his shiny red walker by her with gusto. His hair was pure white and he wore glasses as well as a houndstooth beret perched on his head.

"Well, I have a few aches and pains, but happy to be alive!" His eyes held a glint of mischief as his daughter shook her head and laughed. Her face was pleasantly plump and unlined, even at her age and the tiny glasses that she wore were the same beige color as her hair. The devotion to her father was evident and it was touching to see.

"Dad is doing fairly well, but lately he has been complaining of headaches and blurry vision Dr. Chloe." Darlene bit her lower lip gently and looked at her worried.

"Alright, let's do a full eye exam and go from there. I want to ask some more detailed questions as well. Does that sound okay?" Even though she spoke calmly, Chloe was worried about his symptoms and would most likely refer him to an ophthalmologist. Glaucoma was the first and foremost concern.

"Go ahead, do what you need to do." She measured his visual acuity, checked his pupils and after several more routine tests, ended with the fundoscopic examination. After questioning him further, Chloe asked permission to do more testing including an eye pressure test and dilation. "Yes, that's okay too. I trust you completely with my vison." He sat patiently as she put the drops into his eyes which would help her to see inside of them. Including the retina and optic nerve as well as the blood vessels at the back of his eyes. She really hoped that he wouldn't require any surgery in the near future. She always took that approach last and in only in extreme cases would she recommend it.

"I would like for you to see an ophthalmologist Stanley, so I am going to have Glenda call you with the appointment information early next week."

"What do you think it is Dr. Chloe?" Darlene was worried about her father and Chloe wished that she could put her mind at ease, but she didn't like some of the results of the testing.

"I am not entirely sure, but if it's anything serious, then it is best to have a specialist advise. Please try not to worry, I just want to play it safe." Smiling, she walked them out to the receptionist area.

"Thank you so much for taking such good care of my father. We think that you're the very best!"

Stanley beamed as his daughter spoke and they said their goodbyes. Chloe finished documenting the clinical information along with the test results into his file on the computer. After sending the referral off to a close colleague of hers, she went to see Glenda in the front reception room. Doc Benson had left earlier with his wife for a brief getaway to celebrate their 40th anniversary.

"Any plans for the weekend?" She leaned her elbows on the countertop that surrounded the space and peered over at her.

"Yes, we're going to see the grandchildren on Sunday and we'll be taking them to the zoo for the day." Her eyes lit up when she spoke of them, a twelve-year-old granddaughter and an eight-year-old grandson.

"Sounds wonderful, they should love that!" Chloe was happy for them all. The end of summer was fast approaching and what she always dreaded the most was just around the corner, September. Labor Day to be precise.

"Are you expecting the contractors at your place tomorrow?" She grimaced.

"First thing, the flooring should be completed in the next couple of days. It's a real pain having them in the house, but everything will look so good when it's finished." Chloe loved her privacy so this was very intrusive for her, but she would just have to persevere.

"It's going to be lovely Chloe and if you need anything, please just ask, okay?" Glenda's face was sympathetic and her offer sincere as she reached out to touch her arm. She felt sad knowing Chloe's past; especially how traumatic it was. And she dearly missed her mother Arabella as well.

"Thank you. Enjoy your weekend and I'll see you Monday!" Chloe locked up the office and was happy to rest her mind on the drive home while she listened to her favorite country music. Humming along to some of the songs and then belting out one that she knew the words to. Stopped at the traffic light, she sang the chorus part at the top of her lungs before noticing the man in the car next to her grinning. Blushing, she closed her mouth as he laughed and gave her the thumbs up just as the light turned green. Her home was only minutes from her practice and she sighed with relief upon pulling into the driveway of her charming cottage style home. Most of the time she walked, but she had been running late that morning after talking with her Gran. Her home was quaint, but very spacious with four bedrooms, a big double car garage and a charming yard in Oakville, Ontario just minutes from the waterfront. It was love at first sight when she saw it with the realtor and after going over the asking price by ten thousand dollars, it was hers. She quickly got out of her mid sized electric sedan, leaving it in the driveway and walked up the flagstone pathway lined with colorful perennials to the front door.

With keys in hand, she pulled out the mail from her box and stuck the key into the lock on the charming wooden door partially covered by English ivy. Leaving her purse as well as the envelopes on the hall bowfront chest with the elegantly gold framed mirror above, she figured that she would deal with it later after she ate. Neutral tones of sand, white and copper were being incorporated throughout the décor. The natural materials and light fabrics were beginning to make the home very comfortable along with a big bouquet of delicate white roses resting beautifully in a vase. A keepsake of her mothers, the porcelain urn featured an ornate hand painted pattern. As a small girl, she always loved the delicate bird and butterfly pattern.

She typically brought her lunch and kept snacks at the office to munch on, but she was starving now.

Gazing into her well stocked fridge and not feeling like cooking much, she chose to make an omelette with mushrooms and Swiss cheese. Taking out the ingredients and placing them on the marble countertops, Chloe then put on the television. The handsome news anchorman named Zane Remington, who knew if that was even his real name, with his perfect teeth and equally dazzling smile was on.

"Well, hello handsome!" She tossed her hair and winked at him naughtily. He would stare directly at the camera with his tailored suit and matching tie speaking in his sexy voice, knocking her socks off. Except she wasn't wearing any. She sliced the mushrooms, added a dallop of butter to the frying pan and sauteed them until tender. After she whisked the eggs with gusto and added them to the heated frying pan making a light and fluffy omelette. A sprinkle of feta and a few spinach leaves completed her dinner and she sat down at the big island with a glass of white wine to enjoy. As she ate, she was equally enjoying watching Zane.

She hurriedly rinsed the dishes when she finished, placing them in the dishwasher and carried her wine upstairs to her bedroom to change into something more comfortable. Then, she swung open the

A Gran Scheme

French doors to the balcony off her bedroom that overlooked an amazing view of the waterfront. Lake Ontario with its glorious horizon of yachts, sailboats and picturesque harbours. Chloe sighed blissfully, took another sip of her wine and called her Gran on the tablet. Then, she set it on the stand on the table and waited as it rang. Layla answered momentarily.

"Hi Chloe, how was your day?" Her Gran's lovely face appeared on the screen and immediately Chloe felt happy and peaceful when they spoke. Her pure white shoulder length hair was held back by a tortoise shell clip on each side and one could detect a tiny bit of blush and lipstick that complemented her beauty even more. She and her Gran held a special relationship ever since she was quite young. Even though her family lived almost 3 hours away, they would visit regularly and Chloe would spend many of the weekends with her. Most of the summer holidays also. After that horrific day, she went to live with her in Sarnia permanently. When she left for university, she purchased the tablet for her so that they could see each other when they spoke daily.

"It was fine, busy but productive. How did you enjoy the lawn bowling and swimming earlier?" Her Gran was a member of the local senior's center and kept herself extremely active by participating in many of the activities. She volunteered one day a week at the food bank as well. And at 76 years old, Layla Dawson still walked daily and drove everywhere that she needed to.

"Oh, my goodness! It was very pleasant; I came closest to the target ball and everyone cheered for me as I blushed profusely! And you know how much I relish swimming each day, I always thought your grandpa and I should have put in a pool out back of the house. But, with the beach and Community Center so close, we just didn't feel the need."

"I'm so happy to hear that you enjoyed yourself Gran. What are you up to tomorrow?" Chloe smiled at her.

"Well, I have some gardening to do, reading and then swimming of course. After which, a small group of us are going to meet for tea or coffee. That will be nice, I think." She still held on to her love of reading, always finishing a book or more a week.

"Sounds wonderful! I thought I would come down for a visit on Sunday if you'd like." The flooring contractor was coming early Saturday morning to begin installing the hardwood in the living and dining room. Even though there was so much to do, she didn't want to forgo visiting her

A Gran Scheme

Gran. He promised her that he would come back in the evenings as well to finish. She had only just moved a few weeks ago from her condo and there was so much still to be done. But with her work schedule, it was going much slower than she would have preferred. She took a sip of wine as she savoured the horizon with all of her senses. The lake sparkled against the sky-blue backdrop and many people were taking a stroll along the pathway beside it. Some were walking a dog or pushing a baby stroller and others were leisurely holding hands. The sound of seagulls calling out, complimented the melodic sound of the water.

"That's sweet of you my dear, but I know you're still busy with the house and decorating. Please don't worry about little old me, I want you to get that beautiful home of yours all cozy and finished!"

"Are you sure Gran, you know I would love to see you!" The guilt was flowing through her veins.

"Positive, even though I want to be selfish and have you to myself." She pursed her lips showing the small wrinkles that gathered around them and blew her a big kiss. "Will you show me the view?"

"Of course, but you too, okay?" Chloe laughed and then stood up holding the tablet towards the balcony view showing her the beauty of Lake Ontario. She also had a distant sightline of the Toronto skyline and the CN Tower.

"Wow, that's just lovely! I am mesmerized by it dear and your flowers look divine!" Gran was out on the front porch of her century old 2-story golden brick home sitting comfortably on the diamond lattice settee. She picked up hers showing the view past the parkette across the road to Lake Huron. There were also many boats as well as ships to see as far as the eye would take you. Standing up, she tilted the tablet up the capture both of the Blue Water Bridges that spanned from Sarnia to Port Huron, Michigan. Saving the best for last, a mouth-watering view of the French fry trucks parked underneath with eager people waiting in line. She and Winston purchased their home for a song when they first married and slowly put their loving touch into every room. Faded, but still beautiful damask wallpaper hung elegantly in the great room. And the floral wallpaper with a trellis pattern that they put up together in the bedroom still complemented the rosewood furniture. Special meals were held in the formal dining room with seating for twelve. Apart from some upgrades to the kitchen and bathrooms, most of the home held the same character that they fell in love with.

"Oh Gran, I miss it all so much! Especially you and those famous chips under the bridge of course!" Chloe laughed animatedly thinking of the delicious fry trucks with the vinegar sprayers and big salt shakers. She remembered that on a windy day if you stood to close to the truck window, a mist of vinegar would sting your eyes. Now, their favorite one had a brick-and-mortar restaurant which they frequented often.

"I think that you miss those chips more than me!" Gran scoffed jokingly. Her eyes were teary and there were more creases in the corners than she remembered.

"I love you!" Chloe blew one back and hang up with tears in her eyes. As she sat there in the tranquil setting, she opened up the locket to look at the last photograph of her beloved sister, Ariana. Just 15 years old at the time, her beauty was evident by her long dark brown wavy hair and blue eyes. Mother used to always say that she inherited her grandfather's hair and her father's eyes. It was difficult to believe that almost 13 years had passed since her family was torn apart by the devasting accident when she went to live with her Gran in

Sarnia, Ontario. Her grandpa, Winston Dawson had passed away of a heart attack when she was just 6 years old and that was her first experience with death. She was especially saddened to lose her grandpa, and sat beside her Gran on the hard wooden pew at the church with her face buried in her black woollen dress. She remembered her mother telling her that God had chosen him to go to heaven and crying into the handkerchief. Her family comforted Gran and spent considerable time travelling back and forth from Oakville to see her. She also came to stay with them for the first few weeks after his death. Grandpa had been the head librarian at the local library for many years. He and Gran looked forward to the day when he would retire and they could travel the world as well as spend more time with their family. He had just one more year ironically.

Regrettably, that didn't happen and Gran had to adapt to living on her own and taking care of herself. She never married again; she said that you only find your soul mate once in a lifetime.

Chapter 2

Chloe's grandfather, Winston Dawson was seven years Layla Graham's senior and they met formally one day on her weekly visit to the library. An avid reader and Agatha Christie enthusiast, Layla was on the hunt for more of her brilliant works as Winston gazed at her beauty discreetly, almost in a trance. He had never in his entire life seen anyone so beautiful and delicate with her fair skin, hazel eyes and light brown hair. A fan of Christie also, he conjured up his courage and approached her by asking if he could assist with her finding a book as she looked helplessly at the shelves.

"Can I help you find something?" He was

nervous, but kept his voice from showing it. One hand was in his pocket casually as he stood behind her waiting for her response.

Layla turned around slowly. "Yes, thank you." She told him what she was browsing for and within seconds he adeptly found several of her works and removed them from the shelve for her. Smiling, she accepted each graciously while noting his attire. He wore a plain white shirt under a wool-blend vest with a tiny plaid bow tie under his chin and gray dress pants. Her eyes lifted deliberately to his face which was freshly shaven and handsome enough with brown eyes, his dark hair parted slightly to the side.

"How long have you been reading Agatha Christie?"

"Gosh, several years now, since grade 9. I'm always searching for one that I haven't read and it is certainly becoming more difficult." She bit her lip nervously and blushed when he didn't answer right away. She was wearing a long skirt with a flowery blouse and comfortable shoes. Her gleaming, shoulder length hair was loose except for a hairclip on one side. Her hand seemed to want to brush back the hairs from her face that didn't exist.

"Do you have a favourite book of hers so far?" He seemed to get his voice back.

"I love *Death on the Nile* and *Murder on the Orient Express*." She looked delighted and he smiled at her.

"Excellent, both classic ones. Take a look at those and see if you have read any. I highly recommend *Witness for the Prosecution* as well as *Dead Mans Folly*." He left her then to go back to his desk as she chose the two that he suggested and put the others back on the shelf for another time. She removed her library card from her bag and went to have them checked out by the library assistant at the counter.

"Just these ones dear?" Her glasses were perched on her head and she lowered them to remove the book borrowing cards, carefully writing Layla Graham on each before filing them in the cabinet.

"Yes, thank you." She placed them in her bag and walked the short distance home to her house reminiscing about the librarian. Her mother would have dinner started and if she didn't need her help, then Layla would start reading one of her new books from the library. She had recently celebrated her 20th birthday with her mother, Annette who was single and never married. Her boyfriend at the time had left her when he found out that she was pregnant with her. After going through the whole ordeal alone, she was forever jaded towards men. Although, she did date on a rare occasion, she just never allowed serious relationships to form. Annette was a lovely woman both in looks and personality, but her heart had been broken beyond repair. She was contented and thankful for her only daughter and felt she didn't need a partner.

Layla was working full time at a dental office as a receptionist, but her true ambition was to become a dentist. Not to sit hidden behind a desk taking appointments all day. She just didn't have the heart to tell her mother her dreams; it would destroy her. Layla was all that she had now and to see her only child go out of town to university would tear her apart. And she couldn't afford the costs surrounding the move so she kept her true yearnings locked up inside.

Her hair was slightly messy from the early October breeze on her walk home and her face was flushed. Layla closed her eyes and inhaled the pungent air deeply. It was a robust scent of decaying vegetation which somehow smelled heavenly to her. The leaves were changing to vibrant colors of orange, crimson and gold, clinging to the trees for dear life. Slowly, the branches would release them into the autumn air where they danced in the subtle breeze before resting on the ground. She deliberately trampled through the colorful carpet loving the sound of the leaves crunching beneath her feet as she reached home. She swung open the bright yellow door and called out to her mother as mouth-watering notes of home cooking reached her nostrils.

"Hi mom, what's for dinner?"

"Meatloaf, mashed potatoes and green beans." Her mother looked up cutting the ends off of the green beans and then put the knife down on the cutting board to give her a big hug.

"Sounds so good, do you need my help?" Layla saw that the meatloaf was in the oven, the potatoes were boiling and she had already set the table.

"No, not right now. Go read one of those new books of yours. I'll call you to mash the potatoes, okay?" Her mother knew her strong infatuation with books.

"Thanks mom." Layla went upstairs in the modest two-story home to her bedroom and took out *Dead Man's Folly* to read on her bed. Her room was nice enough, although not fancy at all. The bedspread was the same one that she had all throughout her teens, lavender with little white roses on it. The bed was also host to a dust ruffle and matching pillow shams. An old, white painted desk, described as shabby chic and chair graced one wall. Numerous bookcases holding more books than they were ever supposed to, adorned every nook and cranny of the room. Most looked as if they would topple over and crumble if any of the books were disturbed. Layla had read each one several times over, and some she could most likely recite word for word. She gingerly arranged the pillows behind her head and eagerly became submerged in the murder mystery until she heard her mother call her name at the foot of the stairs.

"Layla, it's time to eat!"

"Coming mom!" Her stomach rumbled and when she looked at the small clock in her

A Gran Scheme

room, she saw that she had been reading for almost 35 minutes. Her eyes were rewarded when she walked into the kitchen and saw that her mother was plating the food for her.

"Mom, why didn't you call me to mash the potatoes?" Her face grimaced.

"It's fine, and I know that you get fully absorbed in a book, so I didn't want to disturb you." Truthfully, her mother did call her and she didn't hear her. But she didn't mind completing the dinner herself, she loved to cook. Both sat down to enjoy and Layla told her about the librarian helping her to find the new books to read. Each Saturday, she walked around the park and by the water before stopping at the library to choose her books.

"That was pleasant of him to mention some of the books to you. Is he a young man?" Her mother was pressing her for the details in what she thought was a casual way, but Layla knew differently.

"Kind of. Maybe late 20's or something." She felt her stomach do a flip and didn't know why.

"Nice. I made a peach cobbler for dessert; we can have it warm with vanilla ice cream."

"My favorite, thanks mom!" She relaxed a little, somewhat relieved that the librarian conversation was behind them. Dinner and dessert were delicious and after she helped her mother tidy up, she went back upstairs to indulge further in her self indulgence. Monday arrived too fast and Layla pulled herself out of bed to be at work for 8:00 a.m. Normally she just had time for a cup of tea and a slice of toast with a pat of strawberry jam so she wouldn't be late. Her mother, a certified nursing assistant, left even earlier to be at the retirement home for her 7:00 a.m. shift. There would be a sandwich for her lunch in the refrigerator and some homemade cookies in a small plastic container on the counter. Annette still thought of her as her little girl, preparing meals for her. Layla thankfully put the egg salad sandwich and chocolate chip cookies along with a Honey Crisp apple in a bigger bag and after brushing her teeth, headed off to work. It was almost a half an hour walk to the office briskly, but she usually enjoyed it unless it was freezing cold or rainy. The dentist was well respected and his patients loved him. Dr. Cromwell was also very nice to work for, gave the staff every holiday off including extra bonuses now and again. She arrived at the attractive brown brick house that had been turned into the practice and smiled as she walked through the glass door.

"Good morning, everyone." Dr. Cromwell returned her smile as did Joyce, his dental assistant. They had come to love her and she was a valued employee as well.

"Good morning, Layla. Did you have a good weekend?" He was wearing his pristine white doctor's coat over his black dress pants and had one hand placed casually in the pocket.

"I had a great weekend, thanks. Lots and lots of reading! And you?"

"Yes, but loads of rest for me!" He chuckled and left Joyce and her to look over the patient list together. It was Joyce's 15th year working for him and she was very efficient.

"It looks like we're super busy today, are you able to stay a bit later if needed?" Joyce looked concerned as she glanced at all of the appointments in the book.

"Of course, just let me know." Most of the time they stayed on schedule, but if an extraction or filling took longer then the office didn't want to reschedule unless they were forced too. The day went by smoothly without Layla having to stay longer than her regular shift. She decided to stop by the library on her way home to return the books that she had read over the weekend. After she checked them back in at the desk, she sauntered over to the shelving to explore more of the titles from her favorite author. She noticed that the head librarian was not at his desk so she chose another book that she hadn't read yet, lingering a little longer than necessary.

"Well, hello! Don't tell me that you finished those other books already." He looked jovial as well as surprised.

"Hi and yes I did!" She smiled wryly at him as she blushed.

"Pretty and a speed reader. I'm impressed!" He cleared his throat.

Layla was flattered. "Thank you for helping me last time and for your recommendations. I loved reading them both."

"You're most welcome. I'm Winston by the way." He extended a long, slender hand.

She held out hers and they shook hands. His felt a bit cool, but nice.

"Layla, and it's nice to meet you." *Goodness*, she was blushing again. But so was he.

"My pleasure. Let's see what you have chosen to read. Ahh, *And Then There Was None*, a magnificent, but brutal tale. Keep the lights on when you read it." He chuckled almost inaudibly.

"I should probably put it back, but thrillers fascinate me so I'll take your advice and keep the lights on!" He left her then to go back to his desk. She noticed that he kept it quite neat and on one side near the corner was a tall glass jar with a cork lid filled with candies wrapped in gold foil. She waved to him as she was leaving and felt her stomach do that funny flip again.

Layla found herself thinking of Winston and his quirkiness a lot. He was right about his advice on the latest book that she chose. It was undeniably thrilling as well as dark, but she loved it. She returned it the following Saturday to the library, even though she had finished it after just a few days. Regretfully, she had been busy. There were a couple of late nights at the dental office and she and her mother spent some special time together shopping and playing board games. They also loved watching the old-fashioned movies together, curled up on the sofa under the hand crocheted throw. This time Winston approached her as soon as she arrived and excitedly held a book out to her.

She reached gingerly for it. "What's this?"

"I have ordered several books from various authors for our library here. This one just came in and I put it aside for you. It's Agatha Christies *The ABC Murders*."

"How wonderful and thoughtful, I haven't read it yet. Thank you so much!" She was flattered by his kindness and taken aback. Her heart fluttered.

"I knew that you would appreciate it." He looked pleased and hesitated as if there was something else, but then he excused himself to go back to his work. After Layla checked out her prized book, she went over to his desk to thank him again. Winston looked up happily with a pen poised in his masculine hand as she approached him.

A Gran Scheme

"I just wanted to say how grateful I am to you for ordering this book." She suddenly felt shy standing in front of him and kept glancing at the candies longingly.

"I loved doing it for you. Would you care for a candy?" His hand immediately lifted the lid off of the jar and he moved it over to her slowly. She reached in and plucked one out before thanking him. Layla had watched him many times discreetly enjoying the hard treat at his desk and she also noticed that he had a tendency to crunch them absent mindedly.

"Well, goodbye Winston." She looked at him bashfully and held onto the candy so hard that it hurt her hand.

"Goodbye Layla." Outside, she looked at the golden wrapped confection as her heart was beating widely in her chest, feeling as though it might leap right out. Should she save it she wondered? To remind her of him? Halfway home, she finally gave in and tore off the wrapper pushing it in her coat pocket and then popped it into her mouth savoring the delicious butterscotch taste thinking about Winston. It lasted until she reached her home, with just a tiny fragment left which she then munched. Removing the gold wrapper from her coat pocket, she took it to her room and smoothed it out before putting it in her memory chest with the other items dear to her heart.

On the following Wednesday while working at the dental office, she was pleasantly surprised when he arrived for his appointment with the dentist. Joyce had made the appointment for him a day earlier when he called to complain about a molar that he was having some pain with.

"Good morning, Winston, I didn't know that you were a patient of Dr. Cromwell's!" Her face was flushed and her eyes were lit up like a Christmas tree. She then found out that his last name was Dawson. *Layla Dawson*, she thought had a nice ring to it and then quickly stopped thinking about it feeling very ashamed.

"I have been for a long time, he's the best! I am afraid that I have been putting off the cleanings due to the fear of cavities. How long have you been working here?" His face also was bright and festive.

"Almost a year. I'm hoping to be a dentist one day." She looked proud as she said it.

His face became demure. "I think that you would make a fabulous dentist." He then went to sit on the brown vinyl chairs in the waiting room until Joyce, the assistant called his name.

"Winston, the dentist will see you now! I really hope that you don't have need a filling." She then took him to the operatory and he sat nervously in the chair as Dr. Cromwell checked his teeth.

"I'm afraid that you have a cavity, Winston. Have you been crunching those confections of yours again?" He clucked his tongue as he asked.

"Yes, I am guilty as charged." No matter how hard he tried, he continuously bit them while he was pre-occupied. After the molar was filled, he went to the main reception to pay and then gathered up his courage and asked Layla out on a date.

"Will you agree to go to dinner and a movie this Saturday night with me?" His mouth was still frozen and his voice was a mere whisper as he held his breath waiting for the answer. There were soft beads of perspiration on his brow and his palms felt sweaty.

Layla's heart skipped a beat; her wildest dream had come true. "I would love to go out with you Winston!" She gave him her home address and telephone number as well and he promised to pick her up at 6:00 p.m. Saturday took forever to come as she waited without patience. Arriving right on the dot in his newer silver toned car, she introduced him to her mother.

"It's my pleasure to meet you, Ms. Graham. Thank you for permitting me to take your daughter on a date." He shook her hand nervously and smiled genuinely at her. He could see that Layla had her mother's beauty and sweet personality.

"Annette please. I'm confident that you will take very good care of her, have fun!" Layla's mother liked him and felt at ease after meeting him. He took her to a casual, but savory diner where they both ordered burgers and fries with thick chocolate milkshakes. Then to a murder mystery movie at the theatre afterwards. It was a memorable evening and they chatted long after the movie was finished until almost midnight when Layla said regrettably that her mother would be worried so she had to go.

"Do you mind if I kiss you goodnight?"

"I would be extremely disappointed if you didn't!" Her voice was soft as she locked eyes with his as he leaned forward and *"boom"* fireworks! It was like a wave of static electricity that shook her entire body. It was their first kiss that evening and the start of a very special relationship.

Chapter 3

Layla and Winston married just six months after their first date with her mothers blessing and purchased their first house together in Point Edward on the waterfront. Dreams of becoming a successful dentist completely vanished and all she longed for was to become a mother herself. Winston was excited for a child as well, but it took many years before she became pregnant. Both were elated and Layla gave up her reception job at the dental office to become a full-time mom. Winston's position as head librarian would carry them financially and he had just received a raise as well.

"How are you feeling my love?" He looked

at her tenderly as he put his hand on her tight, round stomach. It was huge, comparable to a 10-pin bowling ball.

"Tired, but generally well. Can you believe that we'll have a baby in our arms any day now?" Her eyes were like saucers, filled with wonder and excitement. She would deliver the baby in the fall with the changing of the leaves.

"It will be one of the happiest days of my life, after marrying you of course!" He kissed her and caressed her face with the utmost love. Then, carefully, he took her feet and placed them on the stool to elevate them.

"Oh, how you take such good care of me. I love you." She looked contentedly at him.

"I love you, Layla. Thank you for being my wife and carrying our child." He sat down beside her on the sofa and put his arm around her, resting one hand softly on her stomach. His lips met her for a tender kiss. Later that evening, she began to have labor pains and then her water broke. Her suitcase had been packed for a few weeks and Winston anxiously drove her to the hospital worrying excessively about the whole thing. After 14 hours of intense labor, Arabella Pearl Dawson was born. They chose Arabella to honor Winston's mother who died when he was in his early twenties of cancer and Pearl after her mother's middle name. His father passed away of what they call a broken heart just 2 years later and it was such a sad story. Arabella was beautiful and feisty demanding to be fed often. Both fell in love with her right away and Layla's mother Annette was overjoyed to become a grandmother finally. She was a huge help to them and loved to watch her when they went on a date night every so often. When Arabella was two and a half years old, Layla become pregnant again and they were overjoyed to have a sibling for their precious daughter.

It was the middle of summer and they were all enjoying a family day at the beach complete with a picnic basket lunch. Inside, it was filled with sandwiches, cold drinks and watermelon slices. It was hot as well as humid, so they were in and out of the water quite a bit having fun. And they promised Arabella ice cream from the shop around the corner from their home afterwards. Winston was helping his daughter hunt for seashells in the sand as Layla watched happily from her beach chair.

"Look mommy!" She held up a big spiral one in her hand and then put in in her plastic pail.

"How pretty, you're finding so many. We'll fetch you a special box at home to put them all in. And, I'll show you how to make necklaces too!" She got up then to help look for more treasures and felt a sharp pain in her stomach. Gasping, she bent over for a minute and when she stood up, blood was dripping down her legs and parting into thin streaks down to her ankles. She began to hyperventilate.

"Layla, come we need to get you to the hospital immediately!" He kept his voice calm, but was feeling as though he wanted to pass out as he wrapped a towel around her waist and quickly whisked her to the car. Arabella was whining about leaving early and then crying about missing out on ice cream, but she didn't know what was really happening with her poor mother. At the hospital, Winston called Layla's mother to come and take care of Arabella for them She was frightened and worried for her daughter and he promised to call her the moment he knew anything. She picked up her little granddaughter and gave her a big hug.

"Let's go for ice cream sweetie!" She smiled at her, but Annette's eyes held intense worry for her daughter and their unborn child.

"Yay, ice cream! May I have choclate please grandma?" She left out the "o" as she said it and it warmed her heart.

Taking her small hand in hers, she answered. "Chocolate it is. That sounds delicious, let's go get some!" She touched Winston's arm gently as they left the hospital waiting room. Only a short time later, did he receive the devastating news that Layla had miscarried their baby. He wept like a child and then called her mother to give her the terrible news. Also heartbroken, Annette felt empathy for them. After drying his eyes, he tried to put on a brave face and went to console his wife.

"Darling, I'm so sorry!" His tears came quickly again as he sat on the bed and took her into his arms.

"I feel terrible and so sad. Maybe I shouldn't have gone to the beach today, just stayed at home. Or perhaps I did something else wrong?" Her face was deathly pale despite being outside in the sunshine earlier. She learned that she was not quite three months along.

A Gran Scheme

"No, never is this your fault, you mustn't ever believe such a thing!" They talked and cried some more before going home to be with their daughter. It was difficult at first to get pass the emotions of sadness and guilt of losing their baby, but time did heal their hearts slowly.

One and a half years later, they were once again blessed. Layla felt thrilled, but anxious about carrying a baby inside of her and told Winston about her concerns.

"I am so pleased! And we must only have positive thoughts going forward. Are you feeling well?" His heart was dancing.

"Fine, I made a doctors appointment for next week." She was looking radiant and happy. Her visit went well with the doctor and both were relieved to know that mother and child were healthy. When they told Arabella, who was three and a half years old, she jumped for joy.

"I am going to love having a little sister!" she cried happily jumping around the living room. Arabella couldn't wait to share her toys and push the new baby around in the large pram.

"We don't know yet honey, if it will be a boy or a girl." Layla looked lovingly at her. She really didn't mind if it was either one, as long as the baby was healthy.

"That's okay, a baby brother will be fun too!" She ran off singing melodically around the house like a vivid yellow canary. Layla was thankful. The following months went by incredibly fast and her stomach was very large and tight, feeling like it was going to burst like an overfilled balloon. The baby was kicking all of the time and she had just a couple of weeks to go before he or she would arrive into their loving arms.

Layla wasn't quite sure when the kicking ceased, but it alarmed her so she promptly made an appointment with her gynecologist. The office scheduled her for that afternoon when she described her concerns. Winston felt as though all would be fine, not wanting to entertain anything negative so he held her hand as they waited quietly in the examination room. She was lying down and feeling extremely nervous. Both could hear the large clock on the wall ticking the seconds away in the silent room. The automatic sound seemed a hundred times louder than normal and it was hard not to count them. She was dressed in a

A Gran Scheme

sterile medical gown which tied at the back so the doctor could check to see how the baby was doing. Dr. Jordan came in shortly with his female sonographer, who was also rather pleasant.

"Hello you two. I am going to listen to the baby's heartbeat with my fetal stethoscope." The doctor's plump face displayed nothing as he placed the stethoscope on different areas of her stomach and listened intently before speaking with the sonographer. A puzzled look then took over the calmness, causing his thick eyebrows to arch despondently.

"I am having some trouble detecting the heartbeat so we'll perform an ultrasound now." His hands were shaking and he looked visibly upset as he watched the procedure. She carefully applied the cool gel to Layla's taunt stomach and pressed the small hand-held device over specific areas. Layla watched as the young sonographer's face became withdrawn and downcast as she wiped off the gel lightly with paper towel.

"Is the baby okay doctor?" Layla sat up abruptly and was beginning to panic as her husband tried to sooth her.

"I am so sorry, but there is no heartbeat. It would appear by the ultrasound that the cord unfortunately has wrapped itself around the neck of your son causing strangulation." A *"son."* He felt so sad for them.

Layla gasped. "No, please don't tell us that. Why has this happened again? To lose another baby, this time so far along and just before the due date is cruel!" She was crying profusely as was Winston. They clung to each other like both were drowning in a sea of agony. The news was too bitter to digest.

"We don't know why these things happen. One of the most difficult things for parents to deal with and it always breaks my heart." He offered tissues and then wiped his eyes before sitting with them on the end of the examining table.

"What happens next Doctor?" Winston felt dizzy, like he was going to pass out. But he had to remain strong for his wife. It was a true test, but together they would make their way through it, for their daughter as well.

"You have two choices. First, you may go home and allow the labor to begin on its own, usually within two weeks. Second, we can induce labor and within a couple of days the fetus will be born. You may hold him and say your goodbyes then if you wish. The hospital will issue a birth certificate as well so if you have chosen a name, please provide it to them. You will need to also contact the funeral home for arrangements. I will have the support staff come and see you as well if that's okay?"

"I want to be induced, not to have my baby lifeless inside of me for weeks. I can't bear it." Layla was delusional with grief, her eyes lifeless.

Dr. Jordan nodded his head slowly. "I do understand. Let me prescribe the medicine." After he was finished, both were free to leave until her labor began. Never had anything been so hard in their entire lives, not even the previous miscarriage. They leaned on each other and offered support through the difficult time. Layla's mother was there to try to relieve the burden and to take care of her granddaughter, but she too was overcome with sorrow. Because Arabella was so young, they told her that her baby brother was going to live with God in heaven and would not be coming home after all. Her face was crestfallen and filled with disbelief when they gently broke the news to her.

"But why? I want to play with him! Why does God have to take him from us? I don't like him anymore." The tears slid down her round cheeks and she ran into her mother's arms to be consoled.

"I know sweetheart, but sometimes plans go differently and we must accept them even though they make us sad." Layla felt as though her heart had been ripped from her chest as she hugged her only child for dear life.

After a while Arabella stopped crying. "Okay mommy, I understand. Can we go to the park?" She looked so adorable, but Layla didn't know if she could go out feeling the way she was. In the end, she did it for Arabella.

"Yes, let's get daddy and we'll all go for some chips under the bridge and ice cream too, okay?"

"Okay!" She skipped out of the room to the kitchen to call her daddy as Layla tidied her face and brushed her hair for the undesirable outing. She was having mild labor pains, but nothing intolerable yet, only mentally was she struggling. Out at the park, one of the other mother's asked her when her baby was due and that made her break down in tears. Winston answered politely that it would be soon and they left quickly to get their treats. Neither were hungry but watched as Arabella munched on her French fries, dipping each one in loads of ketchup. Licking it off and then dipping it again. When she was finished, she chose her favourite flavor, chocolate or "choclate" ice cream in a waffle cone. Most of it melted down her sundress in the extreme heat, but she enjoyed it nonetheless.

That night, Layla's pains increased and the next day, they drove to the hospital to deliver their baby. Grandma Annette stayed with Arabella while they left for one of the most painful experiences in their lives. Most parents were thrilled for this special time, but it was one of the most dreaded days for them. Lincoln James Dawson was born without breath later that horrible day and they held him as beautiful as he was in the light blue blanket sobbing. He looked as though he could open his eyes at any moment and let out a shrill, but it wasn't going to happen. His hair, a slight patch of fuzz, was the same dark brown as his fathers and both stroked it gently, then kissed his miniature head. Time seemed to stand still as they stared at him through their tears. A soft knock on the door revealed the nurse who, with great compassion asked them if they needed more time. Layla would have taken longer, but it was Winston who gently shook his head *"no"*. She kept the small blue blanket afterwards, holding it tight to her bosom and each felt as though they left a piece of them at the hospital that day as they drove home. She inhaled the scent of the blanket deep into her nostrils aching for their lost son.

The funeral was small as well as somber with just the immediate family solemnly standing in front of the tiny white casket. Afterwards, her mother stayed overnight to help even though she lived just a few blocks away. They all went to church the following Sunday and the service was especially touching with the minister dedicating a portion of it to managing grief and coping with the feelings associated with it. They all said a sweet prayer for the family and they could feel the sympathy as well as support radiating from all of the congregation.

After the heartache of losing the baby as well as the earlier miscarriage, both decided that they weren't strong enough emotionally to try for any more children. Therefore, Arabella was their pride and joy and they doted on her and gave her their full attention. Her 4th birthday was extra special with a celebration fit for a princess complete with pony rides and a magician. Several of the neighbor children were invited to the fall festivities and one had never seen so many faces covered in "choclate" cake!

That Christmas, both were still mourning the child that they lost but still wanted to make it extra special for Arabella. They had just finished putting up the huge assortment of decorations around the house and were to choose a real tree that following weekend. Winston installed the red and green lights on the exterior of the house, standing on a ladder to reach the top. He brought out the black antique sleigh from the garage for the front lawn and then put the grapevine reindeer in front of it. Layla tied big red bows with bells around their necks as their daughter played happily in the snow. She was laying down flapping her arms to make snow angels.

"Layla, what do you think about a pet for Arabella? She has been asking for a dog or cat for ages." He shrugged his shoulders and smiled at her with a twinkle in his eyes.

Smiling back, she agreed with him. "I was actually thinking the same thing! Maybe we should begin with a kitten for her, they may be a little easier to take care of."

Winston winked at her. "A kitten it is then. Perhaps we can all take a trip to the local shelter and let her choose a new furry friend!" He looked so excited and she chuckled.

"Yes, that's a wonderful idea. Why don't we take care of the tree first and then plan for that afterwards." Her heart did that special flip that it always did from the very beginning with him. They hugged each other finishing it off with a long kiss. The ground was covered with a blanket of snow resembling a light, fluffy vanilla frosting when they woke early Saturday morning. It was their family tree outing day. Layla made them a delectable breakfast of buttermilk pancakes slathered in real maple syrup paired with savoury sausages. They enjoyed the meal at the small, round kitchen table with Arabella chatting vivaciously about Christmas and Santa Claus. All the while dripping the sweet concoction down the front of her and onto her lap.

"I'll help clear the dishes mommy." She adeptly carried each plate from the table to the counter where her daddy rinsed and put them into the dishwasher. After Layla put away the syrup and orange juice, they helped Arabella change out of her sticky pyjamas, dressing her in fleecy pants and a purple sweater with a big sequined heart on it. Grandma Annette chose to forgo joining them to choose a tree, but would come over later and help them to decorate it. Glistening snowflakes performed pirouettes in the air and there was a brisk northernly wind. But they dressed accordingly and didn't feel it at all as they hopped around the Christmas tree farm looking for the perfect one. It was already busy with families eagerly looking to decorate like them for the upcoming holidays. The blissful sounds of the seasonal joy could be heard in the children's voices.

"I found one mommy and daddy!" Arabella pointed to the tallest one in the farm and began jumping up and down with glee. Winston looked up at the sky-scraping tree. "Well, it certainly is stunning honey, but I don't think that it will fit in our house. It is too tall!" He scooped her up and kissed her flushed cheeks before setting her back down laughing.

"Come, we'll keep looking. The perfect Christmas tree is here somewhere!" Layla felt her spirits lift as they approached one that they all agreed on. It was a fir tree, about seven ft tall, with very full branches to hang all of their precious ornaments on. After paying, they rode home with it on the roof of their car listening to Christmas music and singing along to all of the merry songs. Arabella's angelic like voice sang Jingle Bells the loudest. Each of them helped to carry it into the house, securing it inside the stand in the living room in front of the big picture window. Grandma Annette arrived shortly after with a large shopping bag, and a bug smile on her face.

"Wow, what a lovely tree!" She hung her coat on the antique hall stand before removing her boots.

"I picked it out grandma. The first one I chose was just too big, so then we found this one!" Her eyes were the size of dinner plates as she ran into her arms with joy.

"You chose the very best one." She was planting kisses on Arabella's cherubic face leaving rose colored lipstick on them. She then took a fresh tissue out of her purse and wiped off the smudges while she giggled with joy. Layla put on some more festive music and then made hot buttered popcorn to enjoy as they hung the numerous ornaments on the tree. Then, they glued paper chains out of different colored construction paper and draped those as well.

"Mommy, can we make popsicle Christmas trees please?" Her eyes were filled with anticipation as she waited for her to answer.

Layla felt her heart soften. "What a terrific idea, I'll get the popsicle sticks as well as some sparkles and paint okay?"

Her face brightened. "Yes, thank you! Grandma, will you help us?"

"You bet. I am going to put tons of sparkles on mine." These times held a special place in her heart.

Squealing with glee, Arabella clapped her hands together. "Me too grandma!" They all worked on the crafts and chatted while they finished the popcorn and then left them to dry. Grandma Annette brought over the shiny green bag with words that Arabella couldn't read.

"What do you have grandma?" She peered curiously into the bag, but the layers of matching green tissue prevented her from seeing anything.

"Come open it and see!" She sat down with her on the big area rug to help.

Arabella dug into the bag with gusto, like she was opening a present on Christmas morning. Inside was a striking Christmas tree decorated with lights and a tiny movable train. She immediately became fascinated and fell in love with it. Annette turned it on for her as it twinkled brightly and began to play the classic songs that she treasured as the train circled around it.

"Oh, grandma, it's so wonderful! Can I keep it in my room mommy?"

"I think that's a perfect place for it. How about on your night table so you can look at it at night before you fall asleep!" Layla looked joyfully at the extraordinary hand-crafted tree that would be always treasured each Christmas.

"Thank you so much grandma! I love it and I love you!" Arabella wrapped her arms around her grandmother and gave her a big kiss on the cheek.

Winston then carried the faded cream-colored box over to the tree and after removing the tattered lid, he gave Arabella the gold star. Then he held her up to place it high on the tree branch. It dazzled and sparkled brilliantly. The antique star had once been his mothers and it not only had a special place in his heart, but at the top of their tree also.

He bent down and picked up the plug. "Okay, now for the countdown. Ready? 3, 2. 1!" Clapping with sheer delight, their tree was now finished.

"It's the most beautiful tree ever!" Arabella's eyes held a look of wonder and that was always the true meaning of Christmas to them. They said their goodbyes to grandma Annette and Arabella waved from the front window to her. Then blew big kisses as she backed out of the driveway.

Layla tried not to think of their lost son and that it would have been his very first Christmas. She couldn't help but to take out his fuzzy, blue blanket when she was alone that afternoon in the house to hold near to her heart. Winston and Arabella were out in the backyard building a snowman and she could hear their voices every so often, along with the squeals of delight. Her tears felt scorching as they slowly released from her eyes and her voice caught the sobs that began uncontrollably. After a few moments, she put the blanket back into the old wooden memory chest and went downstairs to start dinner. They came in shortly after, begging for hot chocolate, which she had already started for them as well. After pouring the rich chocolate concoction into the mugs, she added mounds of whip cream and chocolate shavings before presenting it to them in festive ceramic Santa Claus mugs.

"Thank you, mommy. I love hot chocolate!" Arabella took a big sip and when she smiled, there was a chocolate mustache above her lip. As she enjoyed her treat, they made a shepherd's pie for dinner with freshly baked rolls. Winston loved helping her in the kitchen and was a good cook also.

The following week, they promised Arabella a visit to see Santa Claus at the local department store and she was over the moon with excitement.

A Gran Scheme

"I know exactly what I am going to ask Santa Claus for! But I cannot tell you." She clapped her hands in secrecy and they assumed that it would be a new doll or a kitchen playset as she loved to pretend that she was cooking for them. Dressed in a red velvet dress with a matching headband and cream tights, she looked like a sweet cherub. The dress had crinoline underneath and rustled as she walked, similar to the sound of fall leaves blowing down the road. Overtop, a white faux fur coat kept her warm and toasty. Layla put her black patent shoes in a bag for her to put on when they arrived there, she would wear her boots out in the snow. There was a lineup of eager children when they arrived and Santa was accompanied by his two lively elves who ushered the children to his lap. Then, after telling him what they wished for, they were given a coloring book and a minty candy cane. Finally, after waiting patiently, it was Arabella's turn and she ran up to give Santa a big hug before sitting on his knee to confide in him. His suit was a vivid red, accented with white fur on the cuffs as well as the front. His beard was as fluffy as cotton, his cheeks rosy as McIntosh apples.

His face held an amusement of sort. "Ho, Ho, Ho! And what is your name little girl?" His beard shook along with his stomach when he laughed jovially.

"Hello Santa. My name is Arabella and I'm four years old." The look of sheer marvel radiated from her face and eyes as she gave him another enormous hug.

"And what would you like for Santa to bring you this Christmas?" His white gloved hands touched her small hand as he waited pleasantly for her answer.

After a deep breath, she spoke. "Well Santa, my mommy and daddy have been so sad after God took my baby brother to go live with him. I wondered if you could ask God if he would let him come home to live with us instead. His name is Lincoln and we all miss him very much." Tears filled her eyes as she waited for him to say *"yes"*.

He was touched beyond words grasping for some composure before he spoke. "I truly wish that I could do that for you Arabella, but God has his own plans and we mustn't interfere, I'm so sorry. Can I bring you anything else?" His mustache and beard were adsorbing the tears that had begun to flow.

"Maybe a play kitchen and some chocolate then please?" Disappointment showed in her face, but she would try to be happy. And, she didn't want Santa to think that she was being naughty.

Relieved, he nodded. "Yes, certainly. You're a very nice girl Arabella." The elves came to help her down off his knee and gave her a candy cane and the festive coloring book before she left. She ran to her parents holding the prized treat, her dress making that subtle rustling sound again. They thought that she would want to eat it then, but instead, she took them by surprise with what she asked.

"Mommy and daddy, can I please give my candy cane to Lincoln?" She held the minty treat up with the utmost of love in her eyes.

Layla's breath caught in her throat. "Of course, sweetheart, we'll stop by the cemetery and you can give it to him." She exchanged a loving look with Winston knowing that he felt the same way she did. It began to snow lightly just as they reached Lincoln's resting place and Arabella set the candy cane on top of his small gravestone.

"This is a candy cane Lincoln and it is just for you from Santa. I love you and miss you very much. I'm so sorry that you can't come home with us for Christmas." Feathery snowflakes covered her red wool hat and lined her long eyelashes as she spoke. She looked like a little angel in her elongated, white coat with a pop of red showing at the bottom. Turning, she ran into her mother's arms crying as Winston hugged them both for dear life. After a few moments they left hand in hand to go home, trudging though the freshly fallen snow leaving new sets of footprints through the somber graveyard.

Exactly nine days before Christmas, both Layla and Winston took Arabella to the local shelter for her surprise.

"Why are we coming here daddy?" She looked puzzled as they drove up to the building, not understanding what was inside.

"You'll see soon love." After finding a parking spot, he opened the door for his wife and then Arabella. Walking hand in hand, they entered the reception room and were greeted by one of the staff.

"Well, hello, this must be Arabella!" They had called and spoke with the adoption councillor about their plans and she had been very helpful. She even began the paperwork so that the whole process would be smooth. She bent down in front of Arabella who was stomping the snow from her boots. "I'm Sage, it's so nice to meet you!"

"Hello. Do you know what my surprise is?"

Sage looked amusingly at Arabella's parents. "As a matter of fact, I do! Would you like me to show you?" They had an influx of new kittens arrive in the last few weeks, so there were many choices.

She began jumping up and down excitedly. "Yes, I can't wait!"

"Follow me then!" She led them to a room with many cages and as soon as they walked in, the cats and kittens began to meow. It sounded like a symphony of music harmoniously performed. Delighted, Arabella squealed and ran up to the individual crates. One little kitten reached a paw out carefully to touch her arm and meowed loudly as she stood there peering into the space. She was cream in color with dark brown accents on the tips of her ears and blue eyes.

"Would you like to hold her?" Sage opened the cate door and gently removed the small kitten passing her to Arabella and showing her how to hold it properly.

Sitting down on the floor, she held it close to her face, kissing it while the kitten purred contentedly. "I want this one mommy and daddy please!"

"Why don't you hold some of the other ones before you make your final decision. There are so many to see." Sage wanted for her to be sure. It was a big decision and she was only four years old. Her demeanor reminded her of a child much older; it was rare that a child knew exactly what pet they wanted immediately.

"No, thank you. I love this one!" The kitten continued to purr as she held it protectively in her arms and waited.

Her dad chuckled. "Okay, we have a new kitten then!" He turned to Sage. "What kind of cat is she?

"She's a ragdoll and about five months old. She was found roaming outside and brought in about two weeks ago. Sadly, no one has claimed her. She has been spaded and given the proper shots. And, she is litter trained also. Come and we'll fill in the necessary paperwork." Arabella played with her new kitten while they completed it and afterwards, they took her to her new home.

"Mommy and daddy what will we feed her?" Arabella looked at them worriedly when they walked through the door. "And where will she sleep or go potty?"

"Don't you worry your little head. We took care of that last week and have a supply of food, litter box and a bed for her in my study. And tomorrow we can go out to the pet store and purchase a cat scratching post for her." He left to retrieve the items to show her.

"Hooray, that's wonderful!" She put down her kitten and hugged him before carrying her new pet into the kitchen while she waited for her daddy to come back. Layla filled a small dish with fresh water for it to drink.

He came back quickly with the necessary items and Arabella was ecstatic. The cozy cat bed looked like a little cave with a furball toy hanging from the opening. She placed the kitten inside and it curled up watching them with its vibrant blue eyes.

"She loves it!" Giggling, she peered in lovingly and tapped the furball prompting the kitten to bat at it playfully. Together they filled the litterbox with a shallow amount of litter and placed it in the corner by the kitten's bed. Winston showed her the scoop, how to take out the mess and discard it into the garbage. She wasn't at all disturbed by it, but excited to do it.

"Let's put her in right now and see if she will go." Arabella lifted the kitten out of the little house and put her into the plastic box and waited. "Go potty little kitten please." After a little while, the kitten walked around sniffing and then went pee.

"Good girl! Mommy my kitty went potty."

"Why that's wonderful, she must be very smart." Layla felt happiness again in her heart and admitted that the kitten was just adorable.

Winston stood by his wife and put his arm around her. "What will you name her sweetheart?"

Arabella thought for a minute. "What kind of kitty is she again daddy?"

"A ragdoll."

A Gran Scheme

"Dolly, I will name her Dolly!" She hugged both of them again and thanked them for the best surprise ever.

Chapter 4

Arabella was busy as a little bee all throughout her middle school days. Extremely popular, she had many friends who she met with for visits to the mall or the beach to sunbathe and swim. They also loved riding their bikes through the many parks together and ice skating. She met one of her very best friends, Daisy, when she and a group of friends were walking by her house to the beach one hot, summer day. The humidity was so high that there was a slight haze over the lake which made looking across to Port Huron difficult to see. Sitting on the bottom step to the big front porch of her house with her dog, she watched shyly as they approached. The home was a red brick century home with specially crafted crown molding details and a huge wrap around veranda. Arabella smiled and said hello which prompted her dog, a golden lab to run up to greet them. Excited, it jumped up to lick their faces. Amused, they all bent down to pet the friendly pooch as the young girl looked shocked.

"Oh, I'm so sorry! Stella come on back here now, you're not to jump on people!" Her face was flushed from not only the heat but embarrassment.

"It's okay, we love dogs. Hi Stella! Your dog is really sweet!" Arabella ran her hands over her smooth head and body as the dog wagged its tail with approval and licked her chin.

'I'm Arabella and these are my friends Mia and Sadie." Sadie's freckled face smiled ear to ear as she said *"hello"*. Her hair resembled a bunch of fresh carrots and it was worn in a loose ponytail, tied with a yellow ribbon. Mia, was the exact opposite in her appearance. Long, ebony hair to her waist with a warm complexion. She waved happily.

"My name's Daisy and we just moved in about a month ago." She wore her white blonde hair in braids and looked relieved that they weren't annoyed about her dog jumping all over them.

Arabella remembered the kind older couple that used to live there. Empty nesters, they sold the home to move closer to their grandchildren. They also handed out the very best treat bags for Halloween and always decorated their home to the nines for Christmas.

"We're going to the beach; do you want to join us?"

"Sure, I'll let my mom know. I will need a minute to change and pack up some things." Her face brightened and she looked thrilled.

"No problem, we'll play with Stella while we wait for you." Arabella laughed with the others putting Daisy at ease and she went inside quickly to get ready. When she came out a short while later, she brought ice cream bars and beckoned Stella into the house. They chatted as they walked, eating the frosty treat and that was how she met her very special friend.

"Do you have any pets?" Daisy was curious about the other girls.

A Gran Scheme

Arabella spoke up first. "I have a ragdoll cat named Dolly. She's so playful, I got her when I was just four years old before Christmas." Mia only had a goldfish, which she didn't know if that was really considered a pet, but the others said that it was because it was real and you had to feed it. And Sadie had a dog named Harper who was a Yorkshire Terrier. They played in the water, hunted for seashells and sunbathed the whole afternoon. It was fun getting to know one another better, and forming a special bond between them. She learned that Daisy would be also be attending the same high school in the fall.

Arabella enjoyed her weekly tennis lessons in the summer as well as her figure skating. She had become so good at it, that she had begun to practise year-round when she was 11 years old. Her instructor felt as though she could compete professionally if she wished. Daisy joined figure skating as well and they loved competing in the various competitions in the area, winning many awards. Each composed the agility and grace needed to perform the camel spins and the lutz jumps which were fairly difficult. Her mother carefully framed the medals and hung them on her wall and the shiny trophies graced a bookshelf across from her bed. But Arabella did not aspire to become a professional figure skater. She was ecstatic to be offered a summer job at the optometrist's office in grade 10 and to be one step closer to her dream.

It was bittersweet for her parents when Arabella graduated high school. Her dreams of becoming an optometrist were quickly becoming a reality as she was offered a large scholarship from the University of Waterloo early January. Layla and Winston were heartbroken knowing that their only child would have to move more than 2 hours away to live to obtain her degree, but that was the closest facility.

Initially, she would work towards three-year university science degree including the prerequisite courses to obtain her Bachelor of Science. Then she would be able to apply to the optometry program which was another 3 years. Arabella knew how deeply this would affect them and spoke with them before she applied. She had offered to change her plans. But they wouldn't hear of it, how could they? And they couldn't imagine preventing her from fulfilling her dreams or being selfish enough to keep her there with them. Instead, they supported her and were happy for her.

The delicate conversation was held over her mother's enjoyable homemade meal in early January. One of her very favorites, spaghetti and meatballs with garlic bread and Ceaser salad. She was still on her Christmas break from school, wishing that it would never end. She loved being with them. Arabella pressed her fork in the crisp romaine lettuce and popped it into her mouth, crunching the tasty salad.

"Mom and dad, I know that this isn't what you expected. I seriously don't want for you both to be sad. And I'll come home as often as I can and you'll visit me also. You won't even know that I'm gone." Well, that wasn't true. Her eyes were briming with tears. She had been so excited to receive a response from the university as well as the scholarship, but now she had reservations. Reaching for another piece of the bread, she dipped it into the succulent marinara sauce before taking a bite. It came as a bit of a shock to them because they had hoped that she would change her mind and study something locally. There was a college close by. When their daughter was in grade 2, she did a coloring of herself as an eye doctor, citing that she wanted to be one when she grew up. And she had always been very headstrong, so they shouldn't have doubted it.

"We'll all make the very best of it dear, so don't you fret. You must follow your dreams and we know how much you enjoyed working at the optometrist's office each summer here. Accept the offer, we're certain that you're going to love it!" Her mother's eyes were moist, but she remained strong and optimistic for her daughter's sake.

"I will love it, but I just wish that I could take the both of you along. Maybe we can all move there!" She smiled wistfully at them. "I adore you both so much."

"We love you Arabella and always will." He father got up to hug her then, not wanting to ever let her go. But with any seed he knew, if one never planted it then it would never flourish or grow. Flower or vegetable as a matter of fact and he considered her his very special rose. She helped them clean up the dishes, feeling more light hearted after their talk.

On the last night of her Christmas holidays, they took a casual stroll by the water taking in the jagged build up of ice along the edges. As the boats and ships passed slowly through, they pushed more of the icy matter against the shoreline, causing it to resemble small glaciers. They observed for a bit longer before returning home to watch her mother's favorite, an Agatha Christie movie. Accompanied by a big bowl of hot buttered popcorn and then her father's favorite butterscotch candies, it was a nostalgic evening. When she was little, her daddy told her to savor, don't bite them and she never did, even now. She felt so lucky to have such adoring parents and wished that she could freeze this time forever.

Layla visited with her mother Annette the next day and told her the plans for Arabella. She understood her dreams and was pleased for her granddaughter. Her face was unusually pale and she was shivering, despite having the heat on high and the fireplace roaring. The white cashmere sweater that she wore was buttoned up to the top and her face was flushed.

"Mother, are you okay?" Layla was worried for her. She was usually up and about by this time, not still in her night clothes.

"I'll be fine dear, probably just a cold coming on." She quivered again uncontrollably and then coughed. Flinching, her hand rested on her chest and her breathing labored. Her face was sweaty in spite of feeling cold and Layal could see small beads of perspiration running down her neck.

"I should get you to the doctors right away. Does it hurt?" She brought her mother to the sofa to rest while she made a call.

Nodding, she took a deep breath and winced. "My chest hurts badly. I'm not sure what it could be." She informed Winston at the library and he offered to come with them, but she told him that she would take her.

"Are you sure Layla? I don't mind leaving now to drive you both." He could hear the worry in her voice as she spoke to him and he was concerned. Layla's heart grew. He was always ready to help and support her through anything and she loved him dearly.

"Yes, I will keep in touch and let you know as soon as I hear anything." They hung up and she helped her mother with her coat and then into the car. She decided to bring her to the hospital instead of the doctors as she didn't want to take any chances, especially when she was complaining of chest pains. Her mother was admitted right away at the hospital after describing her symptoms and Layla sat in the waiting room silently praying that her mother would be fine.

"Mrs. Dawson, I'm Dr. Smyth." He was young and held his hand out as she shook it gently. "After running some tests, we now know that your mother has pneumonia. Her heart is fine, but the stabbing pain in her chest is caused by build up of fluids between the pleural membranes which causes inflammation."

"Will she be alright?" Layla was fidgeting with her hands anxiously.

"We have given her intravenous fluids as well as antibiotics. She is also on oxygen therapy to help wit her breathing. She will remain here until her fever reduces and her condition improves, probably about three days." He glanced at his watch quickly and then back at her for any additional questions.

Layla was stunned. "May I see her now doctor?"

"Of course, I'll have one of the nurses show you to her." He left her then to attend to another patient and she stood waiting there, feeling lost. She called Winston from the payphone in the lobby and he insisted on coming right away. After calling Arabella at home and explaining her grandma's situation, he promised that he would bring her to see her the next day. He arrived shortly, straight from the library and the nurse took both of them in to see her.

"Mother, how are you feeling?" She tried not to show how distraught she was with worry.

"It's really hard to breath and my chest hurts. How did I ever contract pneumonia I wonder?" She wore a nasal cannula and a simple face mask with high flow oxygen as well as the intravenous. She had retired from the nursing home months before so she couldn't have contracted anything there. Layla held her hand as Winston brought a wooden chair up to the bed for her to sit on. "I don't know, but try to focus on getting better."

"How long will I have to stay? Did the doctor tell you anything?" She detested hospitals and didn't want to say any longer than she had to.

A Gran Scheme

"Dr. Smyth has estimated 3 to 4 days. The antibiotics should take care of the infection quickly also." They stayed with her for a while longer and Layla promised to return in the morning with Arabella to visit. On the third day after they left, she was bored and walking aimlessly down the halls, back and forth when she heard a low voice.

"Are you training for a marathon?" She turned around to look at the man with an obvious sense of humor. His face looked very amused and he was using a walker and moving at a snail's pace.

Annette kept a straight face and answered. "As a matter of fact, I am." She then put her nose high in the air and started walking away.

"Wait a minute, I was just kidding. My name is Walter and I've just received a knee replacement yesterday, so I envy how fast you can walk." He patted his leg and she could see that it was bandaged. He had gentle eyes and a friendly face.

"My name is Annette and I am recovering from pneumonia, if you can believe that! I rarely ever even get a cold."

He looked sympathetic. "How are you feeling?"

"Fine, I should be going home anytime soon. A knee replacement, that sounds painful."

"Unbelievably so, but I knew it was inevitable. I used to cycle about 10 miles everyday when I was younger and I've been in pain so bad that I had to stop some years ago." The nurse came to take Walter to his physiotherapy so she went back to her room to rest and watch television.

Later on, she saw him again walking slowly down the hallway after she nibbled on her supper which was lukewarm and tasted bland.

"Did you enjoy your dinner?" He chuckled as she shook her head *"no"*.

"What I wouldn't do for a burger right now!"

"Oh, that sounds delicious, my mouth is watering!" She licked her lips at the thought of something more succulent. She sat down on one of the chairs in the lobby and invited him to join her.

"I see that you have a very nice family that comes to visit you."

"Yes, my daughter Layla and son-in-law Winston, as well as my precious granddaughter. She is almost seventeen and her name is Arabella. So bright, she wants to be an eye doctor. Although, she could have also been a professional figure skater." She looked proud as she told him. "You?"

His face clouded over as he nodded. "I have a son Luke and his wife Teresa. Also, a grandson named Nicholas who is twenty-five. They reside in Panama, Florida so I don't get to see them as often as I would have hoped for".

"That must be hard. Arabella is going away to university and we're all at loose ends over that. I can't imagine having family so far away." They chatted some more and then went back to their rooms. Annette was thrilled when they said that they were discharging her later the next day. She felt better knowing that Layla and Winston would be soon arriving to take her home. Before she left, she went to say goodbye to Walter, who was doing the rounds again with his walker.

He hesitated and then spoke. "Would you object to us exchanging telephone numbers Annette? I really quite enjoyed our conversations over the past couple of days. I'm going to miss our banter."

She was caught off guard, but pleasantly so.

"No, that sounds fine." Her face felt hot, but she knew it wasn't from the illness that she was recovering from. She was blushing like a school girl.

Delighted to be back in her own home and comfortable bed, Annette felt like her old self again in a matter of days. She heard from Walter not even a week later and they spoke for over an hour. Enjoying a cup of camomile tea with a spoonful of honey, he told her that they would have to meet when his knee was fully healed. His voice held a glint of mischief and he loved to make her laugh. After a few months, in early spring, he invited her out for coffee and she accepted. They began to see each other more frequently and she broke her own cardinal rule of not getting too close with a man by falling in love with him. Deeply in love really. He was a real hit when she introduced him to everyone and they were pleased that she had finally found someone to share her life with.

Arabella loved her summer job as receptionist at the optometrist's office which she held for three summers before graduating. She would work July and most of August until her move to Waterloo where she had rented a room just minutes from campus. Dr. Allen Parker was kind and a huge mentor to her. He gave her books to read, helped her to understand terms associated with the profession and taught her the names of the equipment used in eye exams.

The summer sped by and on Arabella's last day of her job, they held a farewell party for her. Complete with mini sandwiches and iced sugar cookies in the shape of eye glasses. She was overcome with emotion when they gave her presents on top of everything else. The first was a diagnostic set from Dr. Parker to which she was enormously grateful for and would come in very handy. She couldn't thank him enough.

"Here Arabella, open this one next!" Charlotte the receptionist handed her a pink giftbag with light pink tissue popping out of the top with a card. She opened the sweet card and then reached into the bag disturbing the layers of tissue to pull out a mug. *Worlds Best Optometrist!*

"Oh, my gosh, I love it! Thank you from the bottom of my heart or mug, should I say! My drink will taste twice as nice knowing that this came from you." The last gift, from Celine the optometrist assistant, was a tote bag with a pair of spectacles on it and it was then that she broke down and cried.

"The gifts are wonderful and incredibly thoughtful. I'm going to miss you all so much." They hugged each other and promised to keep in touch often. Charlotte gave her a ride home afterwards and her heart felt full of emotion.

"You're going to do great. You'll settle in and your classes will start to keep you busy. And if you ever need anything, just call me." Charlotte envied her for her courage. She couldn't imagine going off far away by herself to pursue an education or anything for that matter.

"I truly appreciate that, take care." She reached over and gave her one more hug before getting out with her cherished gifts and waving goodbye as she drove away. Anxiety was taking over now and she felt as though she wanted to abandon it all and lock herself in her room to never come out. For several nights, she tossed and turned waking up in a cold sweat, but she overcame it with time thank goodness.

A few days later, Arabella was all packed and ready to go off to university. She felt especially grown up leaving the nest so to speak. Daisy, Mia and Sadie were there to see her off, tears were flowing like water from a tap.

"We love you and wish you all the best Arabella. Or, should we call you Dr. Arabella!" They had all chipped in and gave her a sterling silver BFF necklace and she put it on right away crying. She truly didn't know how she was going to make it without her family and friends around her. "I'll never take this off, it will remind me of both of you, my best friends forever! You mean so much to me and I'll call and write all the time. You back too!" Crying, they all held hands tightly before enveloping into a group hug.

"We promise." They stood on the sidewalk watching them drive away with Arabella waving teary eyed until they were out of sight.

Her parent's car was crammed with all of the things that she would need and more. After they helped her to unpack and get settled, they would go for groceries. Her room was small, but pretty with a kitchenette, tiny fridge and microwave for light cooking. She was really close to the university which was great for walking and using the library. They finished dinner at one of the restaurants near the campus and returned to her room. Her parents seemed reluctant to go and she didn't want them to leave either.

Tearful, Layla asked if there was anything else they could do for her. Her chest felt heavy with sadness.

"You've done so much, thank you for all of your help and support." Arabella hugged her tightly.

"We could stay the night in a hotel if you need us." Winston felt lost at the prospect of leaving his only daughter alone in a strange city.

Arabella forced a smile. "Thanks daddy, but I'll be fine. You go home and take care of Dolly, give her lots of love for me." Her heart was aching, but she didn't want to burden them anymore and knew that it was a long drive back to Sarnia.

Soon, Arabella settled in nicely at the university and met some special friends that she bonded with. She loved her classes as well as her professors and called her parents each day to bring them up to date. She was especially pleased to be offered a part time job at the university as an optician assistant working some early evenings and Saturdays. The income came in handy for some of the extras that she needed and the rest, she saved. It also left her that evening and Sunday to visit her parents.

"Hi mom and dad! Do you miss me terribly as I miss you?" She was being playful and knew that they missed her even more.

"You know we both do sweetheart. How are you doing?" Layla always put the speaker on the phone so she and Winston could both her their daughter's voice.

"Very well. Biochemistry is really interesting, so is physics. And all of my professors are just the best! Oh, and the university has an arena just down the street from my room to practice skating." Her voice radiated excitement that spread deep into their souls as they listened with love.

"That's amazing. We're so happy that you're doing well." They asked about her job then too. She was taking the train home almost every weekend to see them and Saturday evening couldn't come fast enough for them. She also met with her friends for a movie or shopping at the mall. Mia was enrolled in beauty school and she thought that was fitting. Her friend was often trying new hairstyles and always experimenting with her makeup. Her waist length hair was now cut in layers just below her shoulders. Mia also wore more makeup, but looked gorgeous. Daisy was interested in Business Administration so she was taking several courses at Lambton College, which she loved. And Sadie worked full time with her mother who owned a quaint giftshop in town. Arabella made a point to stop in at Dr. Parkers office every so often to chat with Celine and Charlotte, bringing them up to date.

Thanksgiving was the week after next and Arabella was to join them for three days and they were so excited for the extra time with her as a family. She was overjoyed to have a full weekend with her parents and grandma

Annette. They made plans to ice skate, visit Port Huron and schedule a boat cruise on the St. Clair River.

"I've been dreaming about our upcoming Thanksgiving dinner with all of the trimmings. Will you make my favorite chestnut stuffing and apple pie?" Her mouth was watering just thinking about it. The meals that she ate during the week were substandard, quick and without much flavor. She actually flinched when she thought about the cold burgers and reheated pizza.

Her parents were smiling at each other. "Anything for you dear. Let me know what you would like me to make this weekend too." Layla couldn't wait to spoil her with good food and lots of love.

"Thanks mom. shepherds pie please! And dad, I ran out of those butterscotch candies of yours. I have been enjoying them when I do homework or while studying. Will you please get me some more?" She felt tears sting her eyes.

"Absolutely, but you're not crunching them, are you? Remember savor, don't bite it! You'll ruin your teeth." His voice held a note of concern. Layla beamed at him.

Arabella giggled. "No, daddy, never! Give Dolly a cuddle for me please." They spoke for a little while longer planning their next visit and then hung up.

Arabella's parents picked her up on the Friday before Thanksgiving at the train station, they had been waiting eagerly for her for more than an hour. She ran to them as soon as she saw them, with a small suitcase in her hands and a knapsack on her back as well as her figure skating bag.

"I have missed you so much!" She set the suitcase down quickly on the pavement, removed her knapsack and dropped it beside it. Then she wrapped her arms around her mother tightly before moving to hug her father. She never wanted to let go. It felt as though she was floating, she was so happy.

"It's so good to see you dear. Was the train ride, okay?" Her mother's face looked worried, but she looked overjoyed to see her. Both offered to pick her up and bring her back or to purchase a car for her, but she wouldn't hear of it.

Arabella nodded. "Yes, the time flew by, I studied and finished some reading that was assigned."

Her father bent down and picked up the worn suitcase that was once her mothers with the antique floral pattern and brass accents. Arabella put her knapsack back on as they walked to the car with her chatting the whole time about how much she loved her classes. Her eyes danced as she told them about her most recent grades, new friends and the artistic swimming club that she joined.

"Oh, and guess what? I also joined a cheese club! Can you believe it, we actually get to sample cheese! She laughed as she told them about the various types and which one was her favorite along with the "stinky" one that she detested.

Thanksgiving was truly a special time and the moment Arabella walked into the door she ran to hug Dolly who was now a senior cat at fourteen. She purred contentedly as her belly was rubbed and then she meowed softly when it stopped. Grandma Annette joined them along with Walter and it was a jovial time. Her parents outdid themselves with a succulent turkey dinner with all of the trimmings. There was not only the apple pie that she requested, but a pumpkin one as well that Annette baked with love. She enjoyed a sliver of each and felt that she wouldn't be able to move ever again after all that she had eaten. After a brisk walk through the crisp autumn leaves, Walter suggested they all play dominoes around the kitchen table before he and Annette left.

Both her parents joined her at the community ice rink to skate the next day. She had worked so hard on her competitions, that she didn't want to forget her routines. She was also skating twice a week in Waterloo. Both Layla and Winston looked so much in love as they held hands and skated together while she practiced in the centre of the ice.

They were all sorry to see Monday come when Arabella would head back home and even offered to drive her, but she wouldn't impose on them. At the train station, they sat in silence each enjoying a butterscotch candy until they heard the whistle of it approaching.

"Goodbye mom and dad, thank you for such a nice weekend and the yummy food. I loved it all, especially you." She held her voice steady and pressed her eyes closed so that she wouldn't cry.

Both her parents were already crying. "It was a treat having you back Arabella. Stay in touch as much a possible, okay?" Her mother took the hankie that her father offered and pressed it to each eye.

"We love you so much honey." Her father stood back to allow her mother to hug her goodbye. Arabella sat in the tall vinyl seat with the cracked corners looking out the window at them and waved smiling until they were out of sight. Then she put her hands over her face and cried a river of tears. She detested what her choice of education was doing to them and wished sometimes that she would have just stayed on at the optometrist's office in Sarnia for a simpler life. But in her heart, she desired more than that.

Chapter 5

Each of the years she was at school passed quickly for Arabella, but dreadfully slow for Layla and Winston. To them, it was like watching the fine granules of sand in an hourglass slowly sift through the narrow opening. Observing each miniscule grain drop until it accumulated on the bottom. Layla devoted herself to the gardens to keep her occupied and they were most remarkable. Each precious flower that bloomed reminded her of Arabella, beautiful and strong. She had completed her Bachelor of Science and would be moving back home for the summer to work before returning in the fall to the University of Waterloo to begin her Doctor of

Optometry. She had taken her Optometry Admissions Test after her first year and was accepted into the program after just three. The convocation would be held in October and her parents and grandma Annette were looking forward to Arabella formally receiving her Bachelor of Science degree. All they could think about was when she would move back for good to practice optometry where she grew up.

"Congratulations honey, your father and I are so proud of you!" She held the phone up for both she and Winston to talk.

"Thanks mom and dad. I couldn't have done it without your blessing. I'm so thrilled to be coming home for the whole summer." Arabella had recently purchased a car with her savings, pre-owned, but in excellent condition. It was much better driving back and forth to see them than taking the train, which took longer as well.

"It will be the best one in a long time. And Dolly will be pleased to see you!" Layla felt as though a weight had been lifted from her heart, Winston as well. They didn't want to tell her that the house was like a tomb whenever she wasn't there. They both enjoyed each other's company and always indulged in activities together, but their real decadence was their daughter. As soon as her father and mother opened the front door, Arabella ran into their arms and then to caress her beloved cat.

"I missed you so much Dolly! My sweet cat." Dolly purred contentedly and devoured the attention. After unpacking in her room, she went downstairs to help her mother with dinner. Grandma Annette and Walter would be joining them in a bit as well. They had decided on a BBQ dinner of juicy steaks along with baked potatoes to be enjoyed outside on the patio. Winston started the grill as the ladies made some coleslaw and homemade biscuits to go with it. The doorbell rang shortly afterwards and they arrived carrying wine and a large white cardboard box. Inside was a beautifully decorated chocolate cake with colorful flowers made of icing and *"Congratulations"* written on it for Arabella. Walter accepted an ice-cold beer and then went outside to help Winston with the grilling.

"Congratulations sweet granddaughter! This is for you." She put the box on the table and lifted the lid as Arabella squealed in delight.

"Chocolate, my favorite, thanks grandma! I think that we should have this first. Let them eat cake as Marie Antoniette said!" She was serious, but everyone laughed as she dipped her finger in the creamy icing to taste it. The dinner was very entertaining and each enjoyed a slice of chocolate celebratory cake with Arabella's being the biggest. Layla and Winston were in their glory now that she was home. The absence of their daughter was vacuumed from their minds, they were content. She was offered a summertime position once more with Dr. Parker at the optometrist's office which would help with her expenses for school.

As the blistering days transitioned into warm days and cooler nights, the feeling of sadness bred in their blood again. Arabella would be leaving soon to go back to the university, it was inevitable they knew, but they still felt disheartened. It was like old times as she and her parents walked home after enjoying their fries under the bridge. All three were eating big scoops of ice cream in a freshly made waffle cone. Each were laughing and trying to eat it before it melted from the late summer heat and humidity. Layla and Winston finished theirs just as they reached home, Arabella still savoring hers. Upon opening the front door, they saw that Dolly was laying lifeless on the floor by Winston's big, comfortable arm chair. The twisted way that she laid with one paw in the air was alarming. Arabella ran over to her swiftly, dropping what was left of her cone in the entrance way in distress.

Kneeling down, she gingerly reached out to touch her. "Dolly are you alright?" Her fur was still soft like silk, but her body cool to the touch and Arabella began to cry. Her graceful hands cupped her face not wanting to believe that she was gone. Her blue eyes eternally closed. There wouldn't be anymore contented purring or cuddles from her sweet pet and she felt as though she had lost her best friend.

"I'm sorry honey. She lived a good, long life and we adored her for many years." Layla was crying too remembering the first time that they brought her home and how happy her daughter was. That delicate Christmas, she had come into their lives.

Winston carefully picked Dolly up and they wrapped her in a bath towel that Layla brought from the closet. He wept softly as her body was covered up and then her fuzzy little face. Standing there helplessly with her in his arms, he grasped for his words.

"We could put her to rest in the backyard by the forsythia bush that she always loved to rub her whiskers on? Each spring when it blooms its vibrant yellow flowers, we'll be reminded of her." They agreed that it would be a special place for her and Winston went to get the shovel from the shed. Arabella and her mother hugged each other grieving for the kitten that came to them almost sixteen years ago. At a time when their hearts were bruised, Dolly brought companionship and joy and now she was gone forever.

Chloe spoke tearfully. "I don't understand why turtles can live a hundred years and our beloved pets not nearly long enough. It just isn't fair!"

"It's never long enough with something or someone that you love." Layla stroked her hair delicately trying to soothe her daughter. They watched as Winston dug a deep hole near the colorful bush and then they placed her into the grave, slowly covering it with soil. After Winston compacted it, they moved a small concrete cherub from the garden and placed it on top. They held hands and said a small prayer for Dolly. Back inside, Arabella went to clean up the remnants of the ice cream cone that had melted on the hardwood flooring with Layla helping her. The food that she consumed in pleasure earlier now felt heavy in her stomach, making her feel unwell. Almost like she wanted to dispel it and never eat anything pleasurable again. She grieved for Dolly daily with her parents, sitting in front of her small grave until it was time for her to go back to the university.

Her heart was still bruised, but Arabella was enthusiastic to begin her first year of the optometry program at Waterloo. She found her courses on visual neurophysiology, visual optics and clinical techniques fascinating. She also enjoyed learning about the health and diseases of the visual system. She couldn't wait to be able to work with real patients, which would happen in the later years. Juggling her lectures and labs on top of working at the optometry office on campus was definitely challenging. Also, it meant that she didn't visit her parents as much as she desired. They were true saints and drove to see her frequently accommodating her busy schedule. She yearned for the summertime with them and when it finally arrived, it was like new oxygen flowing through her veins.

Her parents had a big surprise when she arrived home one summer after her courses were finished.

"Hi, I'm home! Where is everybody?" Arabella walked down the long hallway and into the kitchen where she saw her mother holding a small kitten.

"Surprise!" Her father was all smiles as her mother handed her the endearing pet.

She took it into her hands and cuddled it. "Who is this cutie?" Her fur was a deep auburn hue which accentuated her green eyes even more.

"The Evan family's cat had a litter of kittens a few months ago and we thought that you would like one. She doesn't have a name yet." Her mother held her breath, maybe it was a bad idea with her studies. Her neighbor said that she could bring the kitten back, but she and Winston would keep it instead.

The small kitten was purring softly. "Really? What a great idea, I love her! What kind of cat is she?"

"Tabby." Her father spoke up.

"I see, then her name will be Tabitha!" Arabella smiled at them, totally smitten with her kitten. Pressing her face deep into the soft, fur and giving her hundreds of kisses.

They both chuckled remembering how she chose the name Dolly after hearing that she was a Ragdoll. They loved her choice of names.

Layla reassured her. "If you find that it is too much to care for her, we can keep her here."

"I think that I will manage just fine and she'll be excellent company for me. She's so precious." Tabitha proved to be an easy kitten and great fun. Her parents had also purchased all of the necessities for her as well including a bed and scratching post. Tabitha even had a little crate for travelling.

They settled in quite nicely together back at her room and she quickly fell in love with the tiny bundle of fur. After a few weeks, Arabella noticed that her appetite was lost one day and she seemed out of sorts. She immediately made an appointment with the veterinarian to have her examined. Tears sprang to her eyes as she put her into the small crate and drove her to the clinic. Fearing something bad, her stomach was tied up in knots as she sat in the waiting room tapping her foot on the floor nervously. There were several other patients there as well including two cats, a bull dog and a small white dog. The Maltese sat calmly in the older lady's lap eyeing the bull dog and all of the felines in the room cautiously.

"Arabella Dawson?" A young man in a white coat called her name. Immediately, she stood up holding the crate and followed him into the examination room. "Hi, I'm doctor Grayson Burke. What seems to be the problem with your cat?"

"She doesn't want to eat and she appears quieter, not as lively now." Arabella wanted to cry, but she wouldn't let herself in front of the doctor and an extremely handsome doctor at that.

"I see, let me examine her and try to determine the cause. I'll then ask you some more questions." He began by listening to her heart and then he felt specific areas of her body. The doctor checked her eyes and then looked into her mouth and throat before he reached for a pair of medical tweezers. In just seconds, he removed a cotton puff that Arabella used to removed her cosmetics and Tabitha began meowing and purring contentedly.

Mortified, she gasped and was immediately ashamed. "Oh, my gosh, how horrible you must think I am! I don't know how she got that, maybe one fell to the floor?"

He laughed. "Kittens can be very mischievous, so don't blame yourself."

"Is she okay then now?" Her face was beet red and it felt like it was on fire. *Gosh, he was good looking!*

"Yes, she'll be just fine. What's her name?" He thought Arabella was the most beautiful young woman that he had ever seen in his life. He just met her but he had never been so attracted to anyone before.

"Tabitha."

He began nodding his head. "Ah, yes of course, like the Tabby breed. Love that!"

"Thanks, it is brilliant, I know." She was flirting with him and liking it. Her heart was fluttering, like it had wings.

"What do you do Arabella?" Grayson loved how her name rolled off of his tongue. He wanted to say it a million times over and over... everyday for the rest of his life.

"I'm in my third year at UW, studying optometry."

He looked very impressed. "Wow, good for you!"

"How long have you been a veterinarian?" She almost said a "*handsome*" veterinarian.

"Just over four years now, I love it very much. Taking care of animals is in my blood, there's nothing I would enjoy more." Except kissing you Arabella he thought brazenly.

"That's truly special. Thank you for helping my little Tabitha, I am so grateful." She held her to her face planting kisses on her head and caressing her soft body as he watched.

He wished that it was him receiving the affection and envisioned her lips on his. "My absolute pleasure. Happy that it was something easy to diagnose."

She put Tabitha back into the crate and started to walk to the door which led to the reception room to pay.

"Wait, I never do this, but would you consider going to dinner with me? There's something about you and I must get to know you better." He had the most attractive looks with his blue eyes and dark blonde hair and Arabella felt the same way.

"Sure, I'd like that very much." After arranging a date for the following Saturday night, she left feeling dazed, but happy. As she waited at the front reception area to pay, Dr. Grayson came out again and told her that the visit was complimentary as the pleasant, older receptionist winked at her and smiled.

"Oh, no, that's not necessary Dr. Burke." Her heart was racing and she could barely think straight with him right beside her. She also didn't want him to think that she owed him anything in return. Or, that she couldn't pay her bill.

"I insist and please call me Grayson. Goodbye Arabella and Tabitha." She watched as he took in his next patient, the large bull dog with a plastic cone around his neck.

Arabella paced nervously in high heels on Saturday evening waiting for him to pick her up for their date. She wore her long hair in loose waves and her makeup was done meticulously. The carefully chosen black cocktail dress complimented her curves and a string of pearls that belonged to her mother graced her neck. She heard him outside of the door before he even knocked. Her heart was pounding and she breathed in slowly through her nose, releasing the air gradually through her mouth. Then, she opened the door leisurely.

"Hi! It's so nice to see you again" She felt like her mouth was frozen and her words were jumbled like a toddler's. Not to mention that her voice sounded three octaves higher than usual.

"Wow! You look fabulous. I love your dress." He couldn't stop staring at her and stood there with a glazed expression on his gorgeous, well chiselled face.

"Thanks, I'll just lock up and then we can go." It took three tries lining up the key to the lock before she finally succeeded, but he didn't seem to notice. He took her to an upscale restaurant that was dimly lit with nice ambience. After discussing wine, he ordered a bottle for them to share. Ollie was mesmerized by her face in the candle light.

"This is really nice. I love the décor and the menu looks so good!" She was considering either the chicken supreme or the salmon.

"You'll love the food, everything is delicious. I think that I am in a steak mood. What about you?" He looked at her amorously from overtop of the menu.

She composed herself quickly. "The salmon actually with the basmati rice looks intriguing." Their server appeared with the bottle of Pino Noir and after opening, poured a small amount in the glass. Grayson nodded after swirling it and then tasting the drink. After pouring for both, the server left and he made a toast.

"To us and to a fantastic evening ahead." He wanted to say life, but held back as they clinked glasses and took a sip. He didn't need the wine; he was drunk on her. All of her, not just her beauty.

"The wine is very good, flavorful."

"I'm glad that you are enjoying it Arabella." There it was again, that name on his lips rolling off like a small pebble down a steep cliff. At that moment, the bread service arrived and they both buttered a section and ate in silence for a moment.

"So, tell me where are you from?" He wanted to know everything that there was to know about her.

"I was born and raised in Sarnia, Ontario. I'm 23 years old. It was only recently for school that I moved to Waterloo. It was daunting to say the least, but I've settled in quite nicely now." She took a deep breath and batted her eyes at him.

"I have never been to Sarnia if you can believe that! I grew up in Victoria, British Columbia and moved to Guelph several years back for Veterinary school." He took another bite of the fresh bread as she asked him another question.

"Is that where your parents are now?"

"Just my dad sadly, my mom ran away to Costa Rica with the milkman when I was five years old. They're now very tanned and incredibly happy." Arabella looked shocked and he smirked, before bursting out in laughter.

"I'm kidding. Sorry, I couldn't help it. Yes, both of my parents live there. I am an only child. And, dare I say, I'm 29 now!" He feigned a shocked expression.

"You have a great sense of humor I see." She couldn't help but to laugh. "I am also an only child, no siblings. Do you see them often?"

"Regrettably, not. Both of my parents had me when they were older and now, they don't travel as much. They're still in Victoria so I fly out about twice a year to visit."

"I see." Their appetizers came and Grayson ate his escargot while she devoured her mixed salad.

"These are awesome. Would you like to try one?" He held one on the end of his fork while she crinkled her face and declined.

Her whole body shivered in disgust. "No, thank you. I will not eat a snail!"

"You've never tried them then?" He looked at her astonished as she shook her head violently.

"Okay, your loss then. What are some of your most favorite meals?"

She thought about it for just a moment. "Homemade, for sure it's the shepherds pie that my parents make. It is so good with creamy mashed potatoes over the beef and vegetables. And, restaurant wise, the fish and chips that we always get under the bridge. What about you?"

"That's easy, pasta. Lasagna or any kind of pasta. I'm a pasta fiend!" He smiled seductively at her and she felt as though her entire body was on fire. *Somebody please call 911,* she thought.

All she could say was. "I like pasta." The server returned to remove their plates and poured more wine into their almost empty glasses. She told them that the mains would be out shortly.

"No hurry at all." Grayson wanted this night to last forever. After finishing the meals and sharing a piece of decadent chocolate cake with vanilla ice cream and a drizzle of hot fudge sauce, they walked back to his car. He opened her door for her and then skipped like a child to the other side to get in.

"I really enjoyed tonight, Arabella. Did you?"

"Yes, more than I ever imagined." Her voice was soft and beckoning him to kiss her.

He leaned over and their lips met like cream in a cup of coffee. There was an explosion, or was it in her mind?

He didn't want to stop, but he was a gentleman so he released her slowly, slightly faint.

"I'd like it if we could go out again soon. Maybe a movie or do you ice skate? The local arena has public skating year-round."

"Yes, to both. Surprise me!" She wanted to run her tongue over her lips and taste his again. The saltiness of the escargot combined with the salmon and wine was like a magic elixir drugging her.

"Okay then, sounds good." They drove back to her place, where he kissed her once more promising to call her soon. Arabella dressed for bed humming the song that played on the radio as Grayson drove her home. Each time that she heard it now, it would remind her of him. Just as she finished brushing her teeth, her phone rang.

"I wanted to call and wish you a goodnight, Arabella. And tell you that I miss you already." His voice was husky sounding.

"I miss you to." Her heart was reckless in her chest, her voice a mere whisper. Never in her life did she have these feelings and emotions inside of her.

"Would you come skating with me tomorrow?" He would always be thankful for cotton puffs now; they led Arabella to him.

"Of course, that sounds amazing. Goodnight Grayson." She slept soundly that night dreaming of the ever handsome and charming veterinarian.

Chapter 6

Grayson called Arabella Sunday morning to finalize their plans for their skating date. She had been fantasizing about him over a cup of herbal tea with lemon when he called.

"Good morning beautiful. How did you sleep?" His voice was silky smooth.

"Very well actually, you?" She didn't tell him that he was in her thoughts all night and morning.

"Good." He wanted to say that it would have been far better if she stayed the night with him, but of course he didn't. "Are you excited to go to the rink? They rent skates, so don't worry about that. And we'll go slow until you pick it up, okay?" Arabella giggled silently to herself and went along with it, not telling him that she had been a figure skater for many years. "Sure, sounds good. What time will you be picking me up then?" They arranged a time and he arrived promptly at her door dressed in snug fitting denim jeans paired with a navy, button down cardigan. Under it she could see a crisp, striped shirt in the same color tones. His hair was neatly combed and his beard was freshly trimmed, not to mention that he smelled heavenly as he gave her a hug.

"You look amazing Arabella." He couldn't take his eyes off of her. She looked like a snow bunny all dressed in white with form fitting leggings, turtleneck and matching vest. Her lips were full and glossy against her porcelain skin driving him mad. Mesmerized, he leaned in to kiss her gently while caressing her shiny mane.

Breathless, she found her voice. "Thank you. And you look exceptionally handsome!"

"Well, I'm glad that you think so. Hey, Tabitha how are you?" He bent down to caress her fur as she rubbed her body on his pant leg, purring. The rink was bustling when they arrived. She chose a pair of white skates in size 7 from the young man at the counter and sat down on the bench with Grayson to put them on. He stood up first and held out his hand to help her onto the rink. There was music playing in the background against the laughter and chatter of the other skaters. Arabella pretended to hang onto him for dear life, trying not to burst out in laughter. She was really enjoying this. After a few moments, she let go and skated with grace and agility to the music. Then, she performed a dance routine that earned her a first-place trophy years ago for him. Taking the beat, tempo and rhythm into consideration, Arabella showcased her fancy footwork. Leading into a camel spin, then an axel before ending with a triple lutz, her impressive show had everyone clapping and cheering.

"Well, I see someone else has a big sense of humor. How in the world did you just do all that?" He was still stunned by her performance.

"I took lessons and competed for many years. I left my figure skates at my parent's place in Sarnia last time after visiting. We still go skating together, even to this day and love the outdoor rinks in the wintertime." She was blushing from all of the attention, but appreciative. She demonstrated some additional moves for him that she knew and then they skated together, holding onto hands. The songs were lively as well as upbeat until a popular love song played. It felt like it was just for them and that's when Arabella fell head over heels in love with Grayson and he with her.

He proposed a mere four months later and she gleefully accepted. Arabella had no idea that the dreamy weekend getaway to Niagara on the Lake in February would hold such a wonderful surprise. After checking into the hotel, both were majestically taken away by horse drawn carriage through the historical town for a romantic tour. The bite of the February air was comforted by the wool blanket that they hid under for the chilly ride. The horse pulling the carriage was as white as the snow and held the pure beauty of a fairytale. Steam escaped periodically from its nostrils as he snorted and trampled down the road. When they returned to their hotel, a fresh bouquet of red roses in a vase and chocolate covered strawberries awaited them in their room.

"Oh, how lovely! Thank you so much for bringing me this weekend Grayson." Arabella's delighted face was still rosy from their outdoor excursion.

"You're most welcome, my beautiful Arabella." She floated into his open arms, kissing him as he held her close, never wanting to let her go. He always made her feel so safe and she loved that about him. Arabella poked her nose delicately into the floral heaven then, drinking the divine scent into her very existence. Next, she plucked a delicacy from the shiny gold box and held it to Grayson's mouth as he took a bite and then fed her one. That evening, they dressed up for a candlelit dinner at the restaurant. He had briefed the management on his agenda for the weekend and everyone was excited for them. The next day was February 14th, Valentine's Day and that was when he was to propose to her. Arabella slept like a log that night with her true love at her side. In the morning, she saw Grayson standing over her smiling in his pajamas with the white robe over them.

"Happy Valentine's Day Arabella!" In his hand he held a small box wrapped in red paper. Arabella felt her heart skip a beat as she reached for it, hoping that it was what she had been dreaming of.

'Happy Valentine's Day! I have something for you also." She got up and went to her small suitcase, moving some items around before producing his and handing it to him shyly.

He was surprised. "For me? Thanks, I'm flattered! Open yours first." She felt as though her heart had stopped beating while tearing off the shiny paper. She opened the black velvet box and suddenly her heart palpitated wildly as she tried desperately not to show disappointment. Inside was a gold bangle with a heart motif on it and she smiled superficially and put it on. Why did she ever think that he was proposing, she wondered?

"It's so beautiful Grayson, thank you. I adore it! Open yours now." His was a silver tie clip with his initials on it and he was very appreciative.

"I'll wear it tonight for dinner!" He kissed her then with all of his love and couldn't wait to ask her to be his wife After brunch, they embarked on a wine tour experience to enjoy. First, they began on a 50-acre grape farm and sampled three impressive ones that tickled their palate. The next, boasted a charcuterie board laden with artisan meats, cheeses and crisps paired with a sparkling rose, pinot grigio, then finishing with a chardonnay. The last winery was Arabella's favorite and included a chocolate tasting flight paired with wines. Each one delighted the senses and Grayson couldn't help but to offer her his sweets after observing her incredible desire for them. Chatting and reminiscing about their day, the old fashioned trolly dropped them off at the hotel. Changing into their swimsuits, they wanted to take advantage of the pool and spa on the property. Their day so far was idyllic and the most important part was still to come. Grayson suddenly felt nervous, his stomach in an uproar.

"Are you ready to go skating now Arabella?" His palms felt sweaty, almost like he was wearing rubber gloves.

"Sure, I'd love that. How cool is it that they have an outdoor rink here!" She dressed in a warm parka and grabbed her skates as well as mittens. He wore his down filled coat and shoved gloves into one of the pockets. He patted the other pocket that held the ring box before reaching for his skates. Holding hands, they trudged through the snowy path to the brightly lit rink. There were heaters set up everywhere with guests sitting by them with hot beverages, enjoying. A warm glow eluded each one giving it a romantic setting. They skated around the rink together before Arabella let go playfully and danced to the music, almost performing for him. As he watched her in a trance-like way, his right hand reached for the box in his coat. Never had he felt this way in his life, like he was floating, incoherent almost. Slowly, he knelt down just as she finished spinning for her to see.

She gasped. "What are you doing?"

"What I wanted to do since the first time that I met you in my office. I never believed in love at first sight, but I do now. It would be my greatest desire to spend the rest of my life with you, have children with you and love you. Arabella Dawson, will you marry me?" His eyes were misty, but so were hers. Arabella's parents adored him and had already given their blessing

"Yes, I will!" She skated into his arms and he picked her up and spun around almost falling onto the ice. Simultaneously, dozens of onlookers lit their hand-held sparklers casting an illusion of gold across the rink. It was nothing short of magical. But the biggest spark was that in her heart.

"Sorry, I guess that means that I can't be your dance partner, only your life partner. I love you." He put the solitaire diamond ring on her finger.

"I love you so much. You have made me so very happy. Thank goodness for cotton puffs!" Both laughed then. She kissed him while the onlookers applauded excitedly for them in sheer happiness and raised their sparklers high into the dark sky. He took her back to their room, showering her with love and pleasure. Her dreams had now come true and she was on cloud nine. Cloud ten if there was such a thing!

Dinner was a spectacular affair complete with numerous courses and wine pairings. Their servers outdid themselves and both felt overly satiated afterwards. He thought that she looked beautiful with the candlelight flickering softly on her porcelain skin, reflecting off of her eyes. Arabella couldn't stop admiring her ring and was in seventh heaven.

"I cannot wait to see the dessert menu. The meal was fantastic, thank you!"

He had other plans first. "It was special, but you're going to have to wait for dessert. Will you come back to the room with me." He had a glint in his eye that made them seem even bluer than they actually were. Arabella looked at him shocked.

"Why, you naughty boy!" She assumed that it was the natural cravings of a man. He asked that she close her eyes when they reached the room and not to peek.

"Okay Arabella, open your eyes." A small table draped in a white cloth with two dainty bamboo chairs was set up in the centre of the room. On top was every type of chocolate dessert possible, including chocolate fondue with cubed pound cake and fruit for dipping. The tiny chocolate cupcakes were decorated with pink frosting and cinnamon hearts. Heart shaped cookies were iced with "I do" on them and petite fours with tiny icing flowers, beckoned to be eaten.

"Oh, my gosh! I think that I just died and went to chocolate heaven. Such a wonderful surprise, thank you!" She couldn't wait to try everything and was sure that she would smell like a cocoa bean for days to come. Grayson dipped fresh fruit and held it for her to eat, kissing the chocolate off of her mouth. Then, he playfully filled up a champagne flute with chocolate for her to drink. And she did, laughing as it left a mustache above her luscious lips.

Their wedding was to take place in December after she earned her Doctor of Optometry degree. She always dreamed of a winter wedding and Grayson was in love with that idea. Arabella's convocation was a joyous affair with her being presented the sought-after Governor General's Academic Medal. She was glowing in the PhD hat and her parents couldn't have been prouder of their beloved daughter. The October day was bright with sunshine providing a tranquil warmth as they posed for photographs. The certificate meant so much to her, but her heart was hopelessly anticipating the day that she would become Grayson's wife.

The day finally arrived that Arabella and Grayson got married. A cold and frosty December afternoon with just a dusting of snow, but neither felt anything but sheer happiness. The small but elegant affair was held in a charming banquet room in Sarnia with just their family and closest friends. Grayson's parents flew in from Victoria and they immediately fell in love with their new daughter-in -law. Arabella thought they both were a true delight to get to know and loved that Grayson's father held a gleam of mischief like his son. Both sets of parents were overly generous and gave them monetary gifts to be used towards their first home together. Grandma Annette and Walter surprised them with the same and they were so very grateful. Layla and Winston were optimistic that both would return to Sarnia to build their life together and start a family.

Chapter 7

The next few months for Arabella and Grayson were a whirlwind. He was offered an associate position in a veterinary office that would be hard to refuse, but it would have its consequences. The practice was in Oakville, which placed them even farther away than Waterloo from her parents.

"Sweetheart, I won't accept the position. I don't want you or your parents to be unhappy." He looked at her sincerely as he said it.

"This is too good to pass up Grayson. And I shouldn't have any problem finding a job there." She looked brave, but inside she was terrified. All she could see in her mind was her parent's face when she told them the news. He took her into his arms and cupped her chin gently bringing her face up to look into her eyes. "That's very unselfish of you Arabella, you're just the best wife ever. Let's think on it okay, I have a little bit of time before I have to let them know."

"Okay." She tried not to allow herself to cry.

Just a week later, it was agreed that Grayson would accept the position and they would be moving to Oakville just a couple of months later. Both decided to tell Layla and Winston in person when they visited on the weekend. He had already called his parents and they were thrilled for him. Arabella was quiet on the drive down to Sarnia and even the anticipation of seeing her parents along with a plate of fries couldn't sooth her. She was picturing their crestfallen faces and she knew the toll that it would take on them. It was early spring and the bursts of color in the gardens and on the trees was beautiful. The pink blossoms of the redbud trees caught her eye and the striking yellow of the forsythia bushes astounded visually. Whenever she saw the forsythia, she was gently reminded of her first pet, Dolly. Pulling up to her parent's house, she noticed that the tulips and the daffodils in the gardens were making a spectacular display of color. The eye-catching shades of purple and yellow praised each other.

"Hello, we're here!" The visit for Arabella was bittersweet and she wasn't looking forward to telling them what they had decided. She knew it would disappoint them immensely.

"Hi, so glad to see you! How was the drive down?" Winston appeared first with Layla right behind him. After an eruption of hugs and kisses, they went to sit in the living room with cups of coffee and tea. She brought in a plate of homemade chocolate chunk cookies warm from the oven for them to enjoy.

"Yummy, these are my favorite, along with grandma Annette's snickerdoodles!" Arabella plucked one off of the plate and took a bite. She placed it down quickly when she thought about the conversation that they would have soon. Her eyes clouded over and her stomach churned.

"Is everything alright honey?" Layla saw the look in her daughter's eyes and was suddenly worried.

"We have something to tell you both and I know that you won't be pleased. Grayson has been offered an associate position with a veterinary office in Oakville and he has accepted." Tears sprang to her eyes and she covered them with her hands as Grayson comforted her.

Winston took a deep breath. "Well, that is good news indeed. Not being further away of course, we will miss you. But this sounds like an incredible opportunity." He was sincere, but disenchanted.

"Yes." Layla piped up. "We don't want you to worry about us. Do what's best for you as a family."

"Are you sure mom and dad?" Arabella was holding her breath and released it slowly through her teeth like a whistle.

"Absolutely, and congratulations Grayson." Winston shook his hand, then hugged him as did Layla.

"Thank you for your support, it means a lot to Arabella and myself." He was feeling especially guilty.

"We'll try to visit every chance that we get. And I can't go too long without fresh cut fries either!" She tried to lighten the mood, but it didn't work for her or her parents regrettably.

They found a lovely home not to far of a drive from each of their work locations. Arabella was fortunate to find a position downtown in a busy optometrist's office. She instantly felt comfortable meeting the staff and Dr. Benson. All were very kind as well as professional and she loved that about them. She and Grayson fell in love with the home as soon as they stopped in front of it. When they stepped inside with the real estate agent, the deal was sealed. The house was situated at the end of a long laneway and gave off a Georgian impression with its symmetry. All brick, the unapologetically traditional home with a pediment supported by two pilasters framing the front door was breathtaking. It wasn't huge by any means, but the high ceilings and cornices made it seem much more so. Three bedrooms for the babies that they would have, it was perfect.

"I love it!" Arabella couldn't contain her excitement.

"Then we will have it. I'll inform the agent that we want to put in an offer today."

The agent was especially pleased, her face said it all. "Of course, will you both meet me at my office in a half an hour and we'll draw up the paperwork?"

"Yes, we really want this house." Grayson was firm in his response letting her know they didn't want to be disappointed.

Later that day, they finally received the news that the home was theirs and they celebrated at one of the new restaurants that they discovered in the area. Fashionably trendy, but with elegant cuisine, Arabella and Grayson indulged in a multi-course dining experience. Clinking champagne flutes several times to toast their new beginning in Oakville.

"Cheers darling. Thank you for buying me my dream home, I'm so pleased!"

Grayson smiled, his love practically exploding for her. "Anything for you my sweet Arabella!" They discussed further, plans for decorating the house and made arrangements to go furniture shopping. They were to take possession in just thirty days and Grayson already had an offer on his condo in Waterloo. Things seemed to be going perfectly for them and the only thing that gnawed at Arabella's stomach was the thought of moving farther away from her mother and father. They would just have to visit them even more in Sarnia, she told herself. Just 2 weeks before the move, Grayson received the devastating news that his parents had been killed in a car crash. Both died instantly when their car swerved off of the road and settled into a ditch. There was mention that maybe his father had a stroke just before the unfathomable accident. They flew out to Victoria, British Columbia to finalized their last requests. Both wished to be cremated and laid to rest beside their parents at a cemetery not far from where they lived. It took several days to handle the funeral as well as the estate and it would take many months before it would be transferred to him along with the funds. Arabella's parents watched Tabitha for them while they were away.

"I can't believe that they're gone. Just the other day, my dad was congratulating me and joking about having a houseful of kids. Now they'll never even see our children." His head was resting in his hands as Arabella stroked his back.

"I know, it's devastating for you. How old were they?"

"Mom was seventy and dad seventy-two years old. I really wish that I would have visited them more now. Time just got away from me. Between school and then work, I should have made the time for them."

"They knew how much that you loved them and they were so proud of you. Please don't feel guilty." He hugged her then for dear life, thankful that he had met someone so wonderful. She took his breath away from the first time she walked into his office and still to the day. Arabella meant the world to him and he was excited to spend his life with her.

"I never want to lose you Arabella. You mean everything to me." He smoothed back her hair and kissed her with his undying love.

Their move to Oakville went without a hitch luckily and the new furniture was to be delivered the next day. It gave them time to begin unpacking the numerous boxes and get settled in. On the granite countertop in the kitchen was a huge bouquet of flowers along with a bottle of wine from the real estate agent wishing both well in their new home.

"Oh, how nice! I'll put these in a vase." Arabella lifted the flowers to her nose and closed her eyes while she inhaled the floral scent. She opened a few boxes before finding the one she wanted with the porcelain vase in it. Intricately hand painted with small delicate flowers and butterflies, it was passed down from her mother to her. It was cocooned in bubble wrap which she carefully unravelled, then breathed a sigh of relief. "Good, it's in perfect condition after the move."

"Great, I think we did a thorough job of packing so there shouldn't be any issues. The flowers look stunning. Why don't we open that wine later and enjoy it with some cheese and crackers?" He winked at her.

Still arranging the blooms in the elaborate urnlike vase, she nodded. "Sounds good. Will you unpack the cooler and put the cold food away in the fridge and freezer for us." She had made sure to purchase some necessities so they wouldn't have to run to the grocery store right away.

"Sure, no problem." He adeptly put away the small amount of food and then moved to help her with the dishes. She told him where to put the glasses, plates and then pots and pans. The two of them worked diligently to empty the boxes, finally stopping at midnight due to exhaustion. Arabella could barely keep her eyes open and her back was starting to ache from all of the lifting. Tabitha was nestled comfortably in her cozy bed after being fed earlier.

"Come honey, let's stop now and have the wine. We can get up early tomorrow and continue." He took her to the island and sat her down on a high-top chair while he opened the wine and poured them both a glass. It was a bright ruby Pinot Noir, very smooth and robust. And after toasting, they both took a sip, enjoying the dry, full-bodied taste. Grayson then went to the refrigerator to retrieve the cheese and pulled out some crackers that she had put away earlier.

"We have an old cheddar and gouda so I'll put that on a plate with the crackers and add some grapes." He arranged everything nicely as though it were for guests and brought it over, sitting with her at the island.

"It looks so good, thank you!" He kissed her, then sliced the cheese thinly and they ate it with the round crackers, finishing the bottle of wine.

"Let's go up to bed." They climbed the stairs wearily holding hands and slept on the mattress. The bedroom suite would arrive tomorrow with the other furniture so this would do for the night. He didn't make love to her knowing how tired they both were, thinking that he would make it up in the morning.

"Good morning sleepyhead!" Arabella stretched melodramatically and sat up as he brought her a tray with tea and toast. "Sorry, we were out of butter so it's plain." He looked disgracefully at her.

Laughing, she thanked him. "I really appreciate this, you're so sweet!" Famished, she finished both slices of the crisp toast with the tea and then giggled as he ravished her body.

"My pleasure. Now, let's christen our new home!"

"My, aren't you a naughty boy! I love you so much Ollie. Thank you making my life so blissful."

Chapter 8

A few months later, Arabella felt nauseous when the aroma of scrambled eggs and coffee teased her nostrils as she walked into the kitchen one morning. She could feel the bile rising in her throat, while running quickly to the washroom. Barely making it in time, she threw up violently.

"Hey, are you okay?" Grayson bent down beside her on the floor in front of the toilet and smoothed back her hair. He grasped it loosely with his hands as she threw up again. Reaching for a bunch of tissue, he gently wiped her mouth.

"I don't know what's wrong, I feel so bad right now." She stood up with his help and filled the glass with water to rinse her mouth out. After brushing her teeth, Grayson helped her back to bed to rest figuring that it was just the flu or something. As Arabella relaxed with him and watched television, a commercial came on for diapers and her eyes widened in shock.

"Oh, my gosh! I haven't had my period in months, since we moved in. I've been feeling fatigued and now morning sickness." She looked thrilled.

Grayson could hardly contain himself. "Babe, are you telling me that we're having a baby?"

"Yes, I must be pregnant!" Neither were ever happier than at her doctor's when they learned that she was twelve weeks along. Overjoyed, they also learned that their baby was due in February. Everyone at Arabella's work was happy for them and Doc Benson promised to work around her doctor's appointments and schedule. Initially, she had been afraid to tell them after only working there for a few months. She decided that she would take a year off to nurture her newborn and then return to the optometry office part time. Fortunately, the pregnancy went very smooth without any issues and Ariana Rose Burke was born on February 14th, Valentine's Day.

"Our love child." Grayson joked as they fawned over her in the delivery room at the hospital.

"She really is beautiful, isn't she?" Ariana was lying on her chest suckling milk from her breast.

"Just like her mother." He marvelled at her strength and agility, thinking that she was so brave during it all. He would have passed out if he had to do it. Mother and baby were to stay in the hospital a couple of days before being released to go home. He had a cot brought into her room so that he could stay with them overnight as well. Ariana was bathed, weighed as well as measured and then returned to her mother. The nurses were attentive, ensuring that both were comfortable and doing well. A huge bouquet of red roses in a crystal vase arrived along with a smaller arrangement in a ceramic baby block container. Grayson took both from the delivery man and placed them on the table beside Arabella's bed. Blooms of light pink and white with baby's breath for their new baby and red roses symbolizing his love to his wife.

"Wow, they are so beautiful! I want to smell them." She leaned into the perfumed heaven breathing deeply and sighing as Grayson held them to her nose. "Mm... thank you!" After he set them down again, he gave her a small wrapped box with a big red bow. Inside made her catch her breath. She raised the 18kt gold locket adorned with diamonds from the opened box as he asked her to open it.

"It holds three photographs, so I thought that you could put photos of me, Ariana and our next child inside. You know, to keep us close to your heart at all times." His eyes were misty as he kissed her. She knew how much he would have loved for his parents to be there, sharing their joy. "Happy Valentine's Day. I love you."

"I am incredibly touched and so in love with you. Thank you, I adore it! But, what about if we have five kids? Or seven!" Amused, he put it around her neck and she couldn't wait to fill it with the photographs.

"Don't despair, I'll buy you another one that holds more!" And he meant it.

A Gran Scheme

"Happy Valentine's Day Grayson." She kissed him with all her passion.

Arabella's parents arrived shortly after with flowers, balloons and tiny outfits for their new granddaughter.

"Congratulations! She is just lovely. How are you feeling Arabella?" Layla hugged her daughter and then took Ariana into her arms, delighted to finally have a grandchild. Winston watched with tears in his eyes as he shook Grayson hand and hugged him, patting him on the back. These moments in life made everything worthwhile.

"Fine, really it was a piece of cake!" She shook her head *"no"* as everyone laughed.

"I know what it's like, and nothing about giving birth resembles cake!" Layla was rolling her eyes. She and Winston were going to say with them to help Arabella with Ariana while Grayson returned to work. They were looking forward to spending time with both. It was a juggle, but Arabella and Grayson managed to balance their work and family life while popping down to Sarnia to visit frequently. Grandma Annette was honored to meet her great granddaughter and fawned over her. Her parents also drove down to see them, sometimes staying for several days. Tabitha, their cat sulked a bit at first. She was used to being doted on and stealing all of the cuddles, but soon adapted nicely to the new addition. Just over a year later, Arabella was expecting again. They found out that she was carrying another girl and were so pleased for a sister for Ariana to play with. This time their baby was born in early spring, a time of beauty and reawakening. Chloe April Burke was a bundle of joy and adored her older sister from a very young age, following her around everywhere since she was able to crawl. The girls treasured their cat and Tabitha returned the affection and was very gentle with them.

When Ariana was six and Chloe four, they moved to their forever home just around the corner from the previous one that they so loved. Much grander, on two acres with a courtyard pool, it still held the same character that she appreciated and the girls wouldn't have to change schools. Their beloved home was just minutes from their work as well. Arabella worked at the optometry office full time while the girls where in school and then three days a week in the summer and on winter holidays. She adored spending time with her girls and savored every moment of being a mother. They loved baking cookies together and she showed them how to make great grandma Annette's snickerdoodle ones. They quickly became a family favorite. Grayson brought home Simon, a Siamese cat after it was brought into the clinic shivering and hungry. His heart was so kind that soon their household contained two cats and one dog named Coco. The girls loved the vibrancy of each and were a big help taking care of the sweet pets.

Ariana and Chloe loved to spend weekends with their grandparents in Sarnia as well, carrying on the many traditions. Each especially loved going for French fries and ice cream under the bridge like their mother did. And Layla and Winston couldn't have been more content having them visit. He shared his favorite butterscotch candies with his granddaughters, reminding them to savor and not to bite them. He read many of the books that he brought home from the library each visit and they treasured them all. But the truly devastating news came when Chloe was just six and Ariana eight years old.

Winston had been outside mowing the lawn and Layla gardening one balmy July afternoon. She went inside to prepare some lemonade with an old recipe that her mother Annette had given her. After placing the pitcher of lemonade and glasses on a tray with freshly baked snickerdoodle cookies, she brought it outside. As she placed it on the patio table, she could hear the lawn mower running out front and went to find him. Suddenly, the engine shut off, cut short like his life at that very moment. But the lawnmower would revive again, unlike him.

"Winston." She called. "Come take a break. I have refreshments for us." As she approached the front yard, her hand flew to her mouth as she gasped.

He was lying face down in the grass beside the mower, the hat he was wearing lay strewn beside his head. Alarmed, she ran to him and turned him over carefully before running into the house to call the paramedics. Trying to hold herself together, she went back outside and checked for a pulse, which was weak. His eyes were closed; beads of perspiration covered his face as she cradled his head between her lined hands.

"Oh, Winston please don't leave me. I love you so much." Laying her head down on his chest, quietly sobbing for him to wake up, she felt like she was dreaming. It was a relief when she heard the ambulance finally pull up into their driveway. The paramedics administered CPR and gave him oxygen. Quickly, they lifted him onto the stretcher and rolled it into the open doors of the ambulance. Layla's close neighbor Anna came over to console her when she heard the sirens and they watched as it drove away with the lights flashing.

Anna put her arm around her friend. "Come Layla, I'll drive you to the hospital."

"I don't know what happened. He was just cutting the grass and then he must have passed out. Was it the heat?"

"It is very warm. Let's pray that he'll be okay." Anna truly hoped so. She and her husband Jordan had been their neighbors for a long time and thought highly of them both. The doctors tried everything to save him, but it was too late, he was already gone. A heart attack, they told her. Layla felt lost without her beloved partner. How to go on without someone who had been by her side for so many years? Arabella received the call from her mother at the optometrist office. Doc Benson relieved her of a patient so that she could take it. Layla was frantic as she explained what happened to her father.

"Oh, mom that's such dreadful news. We're on our way; we'll be there in just a few hours. Do you have a ride home from the hospital?" Arabella was sobbing hysterically. Layla explained that Anna was there with her and would drive her back.

Grayson arrived home from his practice after picking up the Ariana and Chloe from school at almost the same time as Arabella. They were all so heartbroken. Their neighbors Hannah and Owen offered to take care of Coco and feed the cats.

"Why did grandpa die mom?" Chloe was crying along with her sister trying to understand what had happened.

Arabella was trying to be strong, but she couldn't hold back her tears. Grayson took her hand as she spoke.

"The doctors said that he had a heart attack sweetie. His heart wasn't strong enough to beat anymore. God chose him to go to heaven" It was something that her mother had always said to her when she was younger.

"I will miss him so much." Chloe covered her face and cried. Arabella put her arms around her girls to console them. Losing their grandpa was going to be tough on them.

"I'll miss him too mom. What will Gran do now without him?" Ariana was worried, her eyes round.

Arabella sighed. "I don't know, she will come and stay with us and we'll take good care of her."

The drive was relentlessly long as well as somber. They arrived in Sarnia to Layla being comforted by great grandma Annette and several of her neighbors. They offered their condolences once more and left her to be with her family.

"Mom, we're so sorry. We're all very shocked!"

Layla took her handkerchief and dabbed at her eyes. "I can't believe that he's gone. My beloved husband. I feel as though I'm in a bad dream, a haze." She broke down and cried while Arabella and her granddaughters hugged her.

"Is there anything that we can do Layla?" Grayson asked, but he felt helpless.

"Thank you for being here, that's enough." She looked worn and fragile, like she could shatter any second. Annette sat beside also besotted with grief.

The picture of lemonade with the cookies was still out on the table where she had placed it before finding him. Left untouched, instead of enjoyed as it should have been. Oh, how precious life was and how it could change in a minute. The planning of his funeral was difficult and it reminded her of Lincoln, the precious son that they laid to rest so many years ago. Now, her husband would rest there beside him. Two fragile lives lost.

The day of his funeral was bright and sunny, like Winston had always been. The light of their lives. After the liturgy, Chloe and Ariana each placed one of their favorite books that he always read to them with a butterscotch candy on top of his casket. The golden wrapper reflected the suns rays onto the shiny mahogany finish and Layla's mind skipped back to a happier time. With her eyes closed, she saw him sitting at his stately desk in the library. Her mouth curved into a small smile as she reminisced. The way he looked at her as he lifted the lid off of the jar and offered her one of the hard candies. She still had the wrapper in her memory chest to this very day. With Winston's monogrammed handkerchief, she dabbed at her eyes gently and forced herself to reopened them.

"Remember savor, don't bite it! Goodbye grandpa, we love you." Ariana choked on her last words and Chloe reached for her hand. Holding hands, both walked quickly to their parents for consolation as the casket was gently lowered into the ground. Layla smiled through her tears at her precious granddaughters as did their great grandma Annette. She caressed Lincoln's grave with her hand remembering the day that she and Winston held him in their arms. It felt like a lifetime ago, but never long enough to take the hurt away.

Layla spent several weeks with her family in Oakville healing and digesting her husband's untimely death. Then one evening at dinner, she told them that she was ready to go back to her home in Sarnia.

"But mom, we just assumed that you would move here now. To be closer to us." Arabella was surprised at her decision.

"I love you all so much, but I can't infringe on your lives forever. Great grandma Annette is there and Sarnia is my home." Layla had tears in her eyes as she spoke.

"We love having you here Gran. Please stay." Chloe was crushed. She got out of her chair and clutched her tightly, her small body mighty like a bear.

"You'll visit with me and stay the weekends and summer holidays just like you did when grandpa was alive. I'll drive down to visit you as well." They sadly drove her back home on Saturday morning and Chloe wanted to stay with her so she brought her small overnight knapsack. They would meet Sunday afternoon to pick her up and bring her back home. Arabella wanted to visit grandma Annette, so Grayson went directly to the Terrace Meadows nursing home first. Now in her eighties, she seemed fragile, but still very sharp. She knew who everyone was and took great delight in the visit. Months ago, so not to burden Layla, she chose to go into a retirement home when it became overwhelming for her to take care of herself. Sadly, Walter, her companion passed away last year and his family had his body brought back to Florida for burial.

Layla offered to meet Grayson and Arabella in London, Ontario at the end of the visits. Then, they didn't have to drive the full distance when taking the girls back home. They picked a restaurant not far off of the highway where they could have meals together before heading back to each of their homes.

The Burke house was constantly filled with neighbors and friends. Even Doc Benson or Neil as he was also known, his wife Marie and his associate were frequent visitors. The neighborhood was family oriented and bubbling over with kids. They had immediately felt at home as soon as they moved in. Many of the neighbors even brought them welcome gifts such as wine, baked goods and plants. The pool was always animated with laughter and the patio filled with friends enjoying. Grayson would barbeque enough hamburgers and hotdogs to feed an army, telling jokes all the while he cooked. Their friends and guests loved his great sense of humor. After engaging in the meal, Arabella would hand out ice cream treats to the kids as the adults indulged in more beer, wine and lively conversation. The neighborhood was a close knit one and the families all watched out for one another.

Shelley Beer

Ariana was personable and loved by everyone as was Chloe with their sweet personalities. They became best friends with Hope and Oliver next door to them. Hope was the same age as Chloe and her brother the same as Ariana. They often went to the park together, played on the same baseball teams and went skating regularly. Chloe especially loved Oliver's small collection of sand dollars. There were three perfectly shaped ones and she found them fascinating. He told her that he discovered them when he was vacationing with his family in the Florida Keys. He kept them each wrapped securely in a small, hand carved wooden box. Oliver was tall and lanky with sandy blonde hair like his sister, although he was shy. But not around Chloe, he could talk for hours about everything and she loved hearing his stories. Most of the neighbors that had pets brought them to Grayson for veterinary care, trusting him fully with their precious fur babies.

He felt terrible for an elderly client of his that came in for an appointment with his small Yorkshire Terrier. The dog was fourteen years old and like its owner failing in many ways, including having countless decaying teeth.

Otherwise, though the dog was fairly healthy and still robust.

"How bad is it, Doc?" His face showed extreme worry for his beloved pet and his teeth appeared the same as his dogs.

"There are about five teeth that must be extracted. It would involve going under anesthetic and Spark would have to stay the day in our care."

"What would it cost for all of this Doc?" The pain in his eyes was unbearable for Grayson and he didn't want him to worry about finances.

"I want to help you Roger and am willing to adjust the billing. Don't worry about that now." He watched as tears sprang to the old man's eyes.

"No, I couldn't possibly ask you to do that. You have a business to run and a family to feed."

"Allow me a day or two to have Katie draw up the estimate and we'll go from there. Those teeth need to come out for Spark to feel better. Meanwhile, let's schedule the surgery, okay? See Laura on the way out and she will help with that." Grayson would just forget about issuing him an invoice, it didn't feel right to charge him.

"Thank you, I mean that." Roger hugged the small dog and then shook his hand graciously. After he left, Grayson sat in his office looking at x-rays of a dog than came in earlier with a limp. He noticed a slight tremor in his right hand as he studied the notes and believed that it was due to fatigue. His hand shook again as he was typing and alarmed, he massaged it briskly. As he stood up, he suddenly felt dizzy and bent over to regain his balance while holding onto the desk. After removing his medical coat and hanging it in his small closet, Grayson walked out into the reception room. Dr. Michael Cannes, his associate had left earlier along with Tina, the veterinarian technician. The office receptionist was just finishing up with a telephone call.

"I'm off now, have a good night, Laura." She was still completing some appointments for the next day and looked up to answer.

"You too Doctor Burke, see you tomorrow." She immediately went back to her work as he walked out into the parking lot and jumped into his SUV. He was still startled by what happened in his office, and told himself that he just needed to relax for the evening. The music helped him unwind on the drive and he looked forward to being at home with his family as he whistled loudly to a song.

Chapter 9

Layla's mother passed away within months of Winston and it broke her heart to lose two loved ones so close together. Again, they congregated mournfully at the cemetery where Grandma Annette was laid to rest near Winston and the precious baby they had lost so many years ago. Each of them placed one of her favorite flowers with her and said their goodbyes.

"Mommy, why does God take everyone that we love?" Chloe looked at her sadly with giant tears in her eyes.

Arabella pressed her eyes close for a moment before answering. "I truly don't understand why sweetie, but we must remain strong. Let's give each other lots of love, okay?" Chloe and Ariana nodded their heads and ran into her arms.

After pausing at both Lincolns and Winstons resting places, the family held a brief reception at Layla's house. Some of the neighbors as well as staff from the retirement home that cared for her joined them. Later, they baked a batch of snickerdoodle cookies as they shared special stories that each remembered from their hearts. The ate them warm with a glass of cold milk, dunking them as great grandma Annette used to.

The day of Spark's surgery arrived and Roger brought him in as instructed without food or drink. He looked as if he was going to cry as the technician took him in into the back room. He moped around in the waiting room for an hour before finally going back home to wait. Grayson called him personally just before lunch to update him.

"Hello Roger. I wanted to let you know that the surgery went very well. Spark is awake and in the recovery room."

"Thank you, that's great news, Doc! I am so happy to hear that. I was worried all morning." His voice caught and the relief was evident in his gruff, but friendly voice.

"You can come by at 5:00 today to pick him up. He'll be happy to see you." They spoke a few minutes longer about after surgical care for Spark and then hung up.

Roger showed up happily to collect his little terrier at the end of day holding a paper bag in his hand.

"This is for you Doc. I can never thank you enough for taking such good care of Spark. And I insist on paying the bill." It was a large bottle of single malt scotch which Grayson found amusing, but thoughtful.

"I told you that we'll work something out. But right now, Spark needs you to take care of him and give him lots of love. I'll have you bring him back in two weeks for a check up." The technician, Tina handed him over to Roger who with teary eyes hugged his dog close to his heart and kissed him on the head. Still groggy, the little dog's tail wagged with delight. It was days like these that Grayson loved, the ones that were filled with joy. He placed the liquor in the cabinet in his office and welcomed his last patient, a miniature apricot poodle. Honey was there with her owner for an annual check up and exam and in excellent health.

Early the next morning, his first patient of the day, a black labrador was being prepped for surgery. He was just 8 months old and in to be neutered, which was a fairly simple procedure. Grayson administered the anesthesia to the dog and began to operate shortly after. Suddenly, his hand began to shake uncontrollably and he felt off balance. His mind also went blank.

"Grayson, are you alright?" Tina looked alarmed. She took him to sit down in a chair that was against the wall in the operating room. His face had a blank look on it.

"I have to help Spark, he's not moving." She didn't know what he was saying. The lab's name was Charcoal and she was becoming concerned for him. She ran out to speak with Laura at the reception desk to see if Michael was near by. The other veterinarian could then take over for Grayson. When she returned, Grayson had regained his composure and was completing the surgery. After carefully suturing the area, they then carried him to a crate to recover.

"How are you doing Grayson?" Tina's face showed grave concern.

"I'm fine now. I really don't know what happened earlier, but I'll make sure that I get some good rest tonight. I haven't been sleeping the best." He smiled and tried to make light of it, but deep down he was intensely bothered. He knew that some of the symptoms could be associated with Parkinson's disease.

"I'm glad that you're okay." He left her then to clean up the operating room and went back to his office to call Charcoal's owners. It was always a practice of his to contact the owners himself after surgery to update them on their pet's health. After he hung up, his right hand began to shake and he gripped it tightly with his left one. When it didn't stop, he stood up and banged his fist off of the wall. The pain was blinding as he went to the cabinet looking for the scotch. He pulled the textured glass bottle slowly up from the brown bag and twisted off the plastic cap. Reaching for a paper cup from beside the sink, he poured the liquid quickly, noting a peppery scent that was drawn into his nostrils. He threw his head back and drank the contents in one gulp and then poured another. It burned his throat like boiling water as he swallowed. There was blood on the knuckles of his hand as he balled up the paper cup and threw it into the garbage. After washing his hands, he rinsed his mouth out with water and spat it into the sink with disgust. He didn't want to mention any of it to Arabella either as she had just been offered partnership by Doc Benson. The other optometrist had just retired and she couldn't have been be more thrilled. He was so proud and hated to put a damper on her happiness.

When he arrived home, he was greeted by Ariana and Chloe who took him to sit down for dinner with Arabella. Dozens of candles and fresh flowers adorned the table.

"Wow, what's all this?" He inhaled deeply expecting to smell the succulent aroma coming from the casserole dish placed on a trivet on the table. For some strange reason, he couldn't.

Arabella smiled. "The girls wanted to prepare a special meal for us to celebrate my partnership with Doc Benson."

"Yes daddy, we made lasagna with garlic bread. Mommy helped us a bit, but we almost did everything ourselves." Ariana looked proud.

Chloe piped up. "And we have brownies for dessert!" She was ecstatic.

"You girls are the best, thank you!" He observed his hand shaking as he poured a glass of red wine for Arabella and himself. No one seemed to notice, luckily. He lifted his glass high in the air as the girls picked up their milk and raised it with him.

"Cheers to mommy!" They giggled as they clinked all of the glasses and took sips. The girls both had mustaches above their lips. Grayson drank all of his in a couple of gulps and poured more into the glass.

"Let's eat then, it smells incredibly delicious in here." He lied as he rubbed his hands together and served the lasagna from the large ceramic baking dish and added a savoury slice of the garlic bread to each plate.

Arabella was especially touched. "Thank you so much girls for preparing such a wonderful dinner for us and Grayson for your undying support. I would never be where I am today without you.

"I couldn't imagine things any other way. And you don't give yourself enough credit. You are an incredible doctor as well as a mother and wife. You deserve it all." They laughed and joked all through dinner enjoying the succulent food. Grayson finished the bottle of wine with dessert and after the girls went up to bed, he opened another bottle.

"So, are you hoping to get drunk tonight dear?" She watched with amusement as he polished off the second bottle. His hand was shaking as he lifted the last drop to his lips and plopped the glass down on the coffee table.

He looked a bit ashamed at her. "Sorry, honey. I guess I just needed to unwind." The tremor in his right hand couldn't be missed and he tried to hide it.

She looked at him, rather worried. "Is something wrong Grayson?"

He didn't want to break down at that particular moment and ruin her evening. "No, everything's fine Arabella. Come, let's go to bed."

Their tenth wedding anniversary was coming up and he made plans for them to celebrate. Arabella wore a red dress and high heeled silver sandals and he a gray suit as they dined at their favorite restaurant. The chef had designed a tasting menu just for them based on their dining preferences and it did not disappoint. After the third wine pairing, Grayson lifted his glass for a toast.

"Happy anniversary darling Arabella, I love you more and more each day if that's even possible." He took her hand and kissed it, then held both hands in his across the table.

Arabella's face softened. "Happy anniversary Grayson. I love you so very much. You know that right?"

"Of course I do. You have given me such happiness." Before he left for work earlier, he had given her a gift. Inside was a pair of diamond stud earrings and she had gasped with pleasure. Dozens of red roses had been delivered to her at the house in a big crystal vase to surprise her as well. She presented him with a handsome watch which he flaunted on his wrist.

"Thank you for making this day so wonderful. I love the earrings and the roses are lovely." Her hand touched her ears to display the sparkle to him.

"They are lovely on you. You are even more beautiful though. Afterall, I couldn't give you aluminum for our tenth anniversary, could I?" Laughing, she leaned over to kiss him as other guests smiled wistfully at their public show of affection. The evening went perfectly and he was relieved that his tremors didn't haunt him either.

At work, Arabella received the approval from Doc Benson to update the waiting room.

"We haven't renovated in years, do what you feel it needs." He gave her full reins and she was excited to begin the reformation.

"I have so many ideas, you're going to love them!" She was rubbing her hands together thinking about the changes that she would make.

He smiled at her enthusiasm making the crinkles at either side of his eyes more pronounced. "I'm sure that you'll do a splendid job. Promise that you won't paint my office pink though, or purple."

She laughed. "I swear. What about a soft shade of peach?"

He shook his finger at her with exaggeration. "I'm giving you fair warning."

The renovations took just over three weeks to complete, with the contractors' working evenings and most weekends. The transformation was incredible. Subtle changes such as paint and wallpaper on top of new flooring in the patient waiting room made a huge difference. There were new chairs that were functional as well as stylish and glass tables laden with magazines to read. The flooring was carried into each of the three examination rooms and into both of their offices. The wallpaper in the reception area was a vintage bronze embossed damask which complimented the leather chairs in the same tone. She chose elegant artwork for the walls that was both cost effective and eye catching.

Arabella was so excited, she couldn't wait to call her mom. "Hi mom, how are you?" She loved hearing her voice on the other end like she was just around the corner.

"I'm good, what's new there?" Layla had been thrilled to hear about her partnership and knew that she would shine with her new responsibility.

"The renovations are now finished! I can't wait for you to see them. Chloe wants to visit this weekend. And, I would love for you to come and spend some time here as well."

"Yes, that would be nice. Then I can see Ariana, I miss her." She was more of a home body and preferred to be close to her friends so she didn't visit as much as Chloe did.

On a recent treasure hunt to an antique shop in Toronto, Arabella found the perfect desk and chair for her office. A late nineteenth century Louis XV style with bronze mounted figural caryatid ormolu ladies at the shoulders. The matching chair was delicate in looks but held a silent strength that would serve its purpose.

"Oh, my goodness! It's perfect. What do you think Grayson?" Her eyes were as big as saucers.

"I love it honey. It's extremely beautiful like you. Do you want to get it?" He already knew the answer.

Her eyes widened even more. "Really? I would love it for my office."

"Then, it's yours. We'll take it." He loved making her happy.

Ariana and Chloe clapped their hands excitedly. "It's really nice mommy." Chloe was sitting in the chair while Ariana ran her small hands over the bronze ladies.

The shop smiled happily as the sale was quite significant. "Excellent choice. This piece is exceptional, one of a kind." He went to prepare the invoice as they browsed around the shop and admired the exquisite pieces. Arabella stopped at two oil paintings and gasped out loud. Each one was substantially framed in gilt, but it was the girls in both of them that drew her breath.

"The girls in these paintings look so much like Ariana and Chloe, don't they Grayson?"

Skeptical, he turned to look at them. "Wow, it's uncanny! They really do." Each was dressed in a nineteenth century fluffy white dress with pink ribbons and roses decorating the neck. Long ringlets adorned them both, resting on the shoulders.

"I must have these for my office, they're magnificent!" Grayson arranged for everything to be delivered the following Saturday to the clinic. After stopping for a late lunch at a chic restaurant in downtown

Toronto, they drove back to Oakville to feed their pets.

The furniture and paintings for Arabella's new office were delivered as promised early Saturday morning. The movers were careful to a fault when unloading the desk and placed it as per her specifications. Grayson hung the paintings for her on the wall behind her desk. Chloe and Ariana danced around the office and waiting room happily while they put the finishing touches on.

"It's just perfect Grayson, thank you so much!"

He had never seen Arabella happier. "Anything for you." After locking up, they went home and took Coco for a walk to the park. The girls played ball with her as she frolicked about catching it and bringing it back. After running around, Grayson's body felt stiff and he knew that it was also a symptom of Parkinson's disease.

A few weeks later, Arabella saw his hand shaking again as they ate dinner. It was frequent now as was the drinking.

"Grayson, I think that we should talk later." She didn't want to alarm the girls or discuss what was on her mind in front of them.

His face was masklike as he nodded his head slowly. After the girls were settled in bed reading, she sat with him on the sofa.

"I feel as though you're not telling me something. What is it, talk to me!" Her eyes beckoned honesty.

He took her hand and held it against his face as he spoke. "I think that I have Parkinson's disease."

"Have you seen a doctor?" She tried not to show the fear that she felt inside.

"No, I would never do that without telling you first. I guess that I'm in denial, really. Maybe if I didn't address it, then it would go away. I wanted to tell you, but I just kept putting it off with your partnership and everything else."

"That's crazy, we have to get a diagnosis and help for you. I can't bear the thought of you suffering." She was crying openly thinking about his struggles and how he had to go through it alone. They called the doctor the very next morning and they squeezed him in just a day later. Arabella held his hand firmly as their family doctor asked him various questions about his health. After explaining his symptoms, Grayson was told that he would be referred to a neurologist. The appointment was still weeks away and following an extensive list of procedures and testing, it still wasn't conclusive.

Arabella was there to support him no matter what and would always be. There were good days and not so good days. Sadly, they lost Tabitha and it was a blow to all of them. The sweet cat that brought Arabella and Grayson together so many years ago had passed away from cancer. He did everything that he could, knowing how special she was to his family and even asked a specialist that he knew to help. But nothing could save her and when she died, he felt an even bigger loss in the form of guilt. Now it was just Simon the cat and Coco. He was angry all of the time, snapping at her and the girls which was disheartening to Arabella. Never had she seen this side to her husband before and she felt helpless.

Canada Day was a giant celebration on their street and they were hosting it at their home that year. An affair that was talked about for weeks after included spectacular food, drinks and fireworks that rivaled most. It was potluck style and each of the invitees brought a special dish to share on top of the grill foods. Endless salads, sides and desserts were enough to make anyone's mouth water. Now ten and twelve, Chloe and Ariana were helping Arabella with the red and white decorations. There were dozens of flags as well as balloons and banners to be hung on the fence. When they finished that, Arabella assigned new duties.

"Ariana, will you set the tables please? There are plates and plastic cutlery including napkins inside on the countertop" They had the rental company set up additional tables and chairs around the yard to accommodate all of the guests. Each one was covered with either a red or white tablecloth.

"Sure mom, right away." She was tall and very delicate, her dark brown hair cascading down her back. But it was the combination of her piercing blue eyes in contrast with her hair which captivated people. Ariana's features were flawless and many said that she should become a model. But she wasn't into hair or makeup and was more interested in becoming a veterinarian like her father. Her empathy for the pets was incredible with her dad calling her the animal whisperer. She loved helping him at the clinic and bore the kind of compassion that owners looked for when choosing a vet. She was also personable and outgoing. Chloe, on the other hand was a sweet soul, soft spoken and delicate. Smart as well, she could be anything that she wanted to be later in life.

"What can I do next." She looked at her mom with wide eyes and Arabella couldn't help but reach out and touch her shoulder length chestnut hair. She had inherited her mother's looks including her hazel eyes and even Arabella saw herself in her.

"Come help me bring the drinks out to the outdoor kitchen." Together they worked as Grayson prepared the meats for the barbeque. It wasn't long before the guests began to stream into their backyard and the party was soon in full swing. Owen and Hannah, their next-door neighbors brought homemade apple pies that Hope and her brother Oliver carried. She was ten and her brother had just turned twelve also.

"Yummy, my favorite! Let's put them on the dessert table for later, or maybe I'll eat a piece now." Grayson joked and then laughed as he placed them with the cookies, cakes and other desserts. They ran off to play badminton and games with the other kids. Some of the neighbors were frolicking in the water, others relaxing on pool loungers with margaritas.

"What can I offer you to drink Hannah?" Grayson's mouth couldn't wait to taste a beer.

"I'd like a glass of white wine please." She thanked him as he poured it and handed it to her.

"Beer for me, thanks." Owen took a long sip from the can as he complimented Arabella on the decorations.

"Thank you. The girls were a huge help as well." They went on to mix and mingle with the other neighbours while Grayson fired up the grill. He noticed again, the tremor in his right hand and closed the lid after flipping the burgers and sausages. They had been getting worse and he had been drinking more to deal with it. He drank the beer and then made himself a strong drink, finishing it in barely a gulp. Then another. At dusk, they handed out sparklers which always reminded Arabella of the night when Grayson proposed to her in Niagara on the Lake. He smiled at her with the most powerful love in his eyes when they were lit and glowing against the dark sky.

"I love you sweet Arabella." He stole a kiss from her and held her tightly as they watched the fun. She could smell the strong liquor on his lips, knowing that he used it as medicine to help him cope. Oliver and Chloe ran through the yard making spiral shapes with theirs as the others shouted. Later, they all moved their folding chairs to the front cul-de-sac area of their street to watch the brilliant display of fireworks. Bursts of intense color lit up the night sky, cascading into eye popping entertainment. The next day, the neighbors came back to help clean up the mess from the night before, fondly recalling all of the fun they had.

It was losing a faithful client's pet on the operating table that was the final blow. Grayson was drinking excessively now to manage the symptoms that he was having. Because he was slightly impaired, he had given the small dog an elevated amount of anesthesia by accident. She went into respiratory cessation and died on the operating table while they worked feverishly to save her. He never forgave himself and a deep, dark depression gripped him. His associate Michael took over added responsibility leaving him to the basic care such as vaccinations and annual checkups. It was a blow to his ego that he couldn't deal with and he resented that his health had been threatened that way. Issuing heartworm medications and antibiotics wasn't why he went into veterinary care.

As a few more years passed, Grayson spent more and more time at home drinking. He was also having trouble sleeping at night, getting up from the bed to pace for hours.

The tiniest of things upset him and they eventually stopped having parties at their home or going out. Their friends and neighbors also noticed the difference in his personality and were worried for him. It was embarrassing for Arabella to watch him drink too much and then explode over nothing in front of their guests. While sitting together watching a movie one evening, he had a terrible fit of rage. Slamming his drink down so hard, it startled them.

"Damn it, Ariana. Put that phone away and stop talking, I can't hear what they're even saying!" His voice didn't sound like his own and it was unbelievably disturbing.

A Gran Scheme

"What's wrong with you dad? All you do is yell all of the time and drink. You never used to be like this." She stormed upstairs to her room leaving Arabella at her wits end. Chloe was at her Gran's visiting and she was relieved that she wasn't there to witness his outbursts. She noticed the tremors now daily and knew that he was having trouble dealing with them.

"You didn't have to treat her that way Grayson. She's only a teenager. Can't you stop drinking so much and try to be nicer? Your self pity is not helping, let's find a way to manage all of this in a more productive way." She moved over to hug him, but he pushed her away. Never had he done that.

"Easy for you to say, my career is over." He got up and went to the kitchen to take a bottle of red wine from the cupboard without a glass. He carried to his study to drink it in peace.

Chapter 10

Chloe looked forward to spending as much time with her Gran in Sarnia as possible. The summers were the absolute best and she loved to help with the gardens around her home. The flower beds lined the front and backyard with an impressive assortment of bulbs, annuals and perennials. They were planted with careful consideration over the years to feature blooms from early spring right into the fall. All of the flowers seemed to be competing to be the star of the show. She especially admired the strength and beauty of the primrose which was the first to bloom in the spring. One could find colors of pink, yellow and red peeking through the snow even before the crocus or daffodils. The blooms were resilient to the cold, making them one of the hardiest perennials. Presently, clusters of black eyed Susans basked in the late summer sunshine with their dark yellow petals. Joining them were lavender and phlox with a complimentary spray of hydrangeas boasting huge cone shape flowers. To the rear of the backyard, an extensive vegetable bed nurtured various types of vegetables.

It was almost the end of August and Chloe was spending the last of her summer holidays with her Gran. She had even brought Coco for a visit and she was basking in the sun on her back porch. The chocolate lab had become very attached so she went almost everywhere with her. They had spent many of the weeks throughout the summer baking and tending to the gardens. Both went strawberry picking and had made jam in June also. Gran found it amusing to see Chloe stuffing the fresh berries into her mouth as she collected them, her lips red like she was wearing lipstick. Now, they were happily reaping the rewards of the vegetables that they started from seeds in early May. In between the rows were clusters of marigolds to stave away the aphids as well as lavender to repel other bugs.

"Gran, look at all of the carrots, tomatoes and cucumbers in my basket!" She wore pink garden gloves with red hearts on them as she showed her.

She smiled lovingly at her granddaughter. "Oh, my! We certainly have plenty, don't we? You'll take home a bunch and we'll give some away to Anna and our other neighbors. I'll also show you how to can the tomatoes, make pickles and freeze the carrots!"

"I'd love that. Is it difficult to do?" Chloe reminded her so much of her Arabella at that age, always cheerful with a genuine desire to learn. Her chestnut hair was tied back loosely in a ponytail, but the tendrils that came loose framed her face. Every once and a while, a gentle breeze lifted them up, twirling each in the air.

Gran smiled at her. "No, but it does require work. Nothing good is ever easy." She continued to pick potatoes, pulling them up by the stems and shaking off the dirt. Her wicker basket was full as well. "What do you say we put all of this inside and take a break. We could go have some chips under the bridge and ice cream."

Chloe's face lit up and her hazel eyes widened. "Yes, that sounds great, I am so hungry after all of this hard work! Although, I just loved it Gran." They brought in the baskets, setting them on the large kitchen table and then went to clean up. Chloe fed Coco and gave her a treat which she happily settled down with on her bed.

When they returned, she and Gran blanched the carrots, put them in an ice bath and then froze them in plastic bags. After that, they prepared the jars in a water bath to sterilize them for the tomatoes. She showed Chloe how to score the tomatoes on the bottom before placing them in the boiling water. After about thirty seconds, they scooped them out carefully and placed them in ice water. The skin peeled off easily and then they sliced them after removing the core.

"What's next Gran? Do we put them in a jar now?"

"Not yet, we must cook them next. After they reach a boil, then we'll simmer them for about five minutes or so. Then they'll be ready for the jars." As Chloe stirred the big pot of tomatoes, she got the tongs out and dampened a dishcloth to set them on. After filling each one with a small amount of lemon juice and the tomato mixture she placed the lids on.

"Now are they finished?" Chloe was anxious to move on to the next job.

"Almost. Now we're going to process the jars in boiling water for forty-five minutes, then they'll be done!"

"Are we going to make the pickles tonight, Gran?"

She looked lovingly at her granddaughter. "No, that's enough hard work for today. Why don't we make pasta for dinner and then watch a movie together? But first, let's take Coco for a walk." Chloe nodded her approval. They tidied up the kitchen and put the canned goods on the shelf in the pantry. Gran kept some jars in a box for her to take home along with the potatoes, fresh carrots and tomatoes.

The next day they even managed to make bread and butter style pickles from the English cucumbers that Chloe loved. After that, they packed up a care box for Anna, Gran's neighbor and carried it over to her house. She had lost her husband last year and now lived alone. Her son lived overseas and only visited a few times a year, so she valued the visits from Layla and Chloe.

"Why, what's all this?" Anna's hand flew to her throat. She was pleasantly surprised and very grateful.

Chloe chirped up happily. "We made strawberry jam, canned tomatoes and pickles. Oh, and there are some fresh carrots, tomatoes and potatoes for you! I helped Gran pick it from the garden and then make all of it."

"You're a good helper. Thank you so much for thinking of me. Come in, I have some chocolate cupcakes that I just made. Would you like one?" She winked at Layla who smiled back at her.

Arabella practically jumped for joy. "Yes, please. Chocolate cupcakes are my very favorite!"

"Wonderful, follow me then. I'll put on some tea for us Layla. It looks like by the all of the goodies in this box, that you both have been working non-stop!" Layla set the box down onto the countertop with Anna's help.

Layla nodded. "Yes, and tea sounds lovely Anna." They sat at her table in the cheery yellow kitchen chatting about Felix, her son and the latest news from the community centre that they attended.

With just days before school was to start up again, Gran planned a special outing for them on the Sunday before Labor Day. The sightseeing boat cruise toured the St. Clair River and offered guests a brunch to enjoy while taking in the view. She knew that Chloe was apprehensive about leaving and wanted to make her last full day special. The next morning after that, they were going to meet Arabella, Grayson and Ariana at the restaurant outside of London. It would be just an hour's drive for her, but a couple of hours for the family. But it still shortened their time driving and they were grateful. Layla knew that there were issues between them and her heart went out to both. Arabella had confided to her during one of their conversations and she offered to come and stay to help. But unfortunately, there was very little that she could do.

That evening in Oakville, Arabella hummed in the kitchen as she made a Sunday supper of prime rib with au jus and mashed potatoes paired with assorted vegetables. She rolled out the dough for the apple pie and laid it in the deep-dish plate. Using a paring knife, she peeled the skin from the apples, then cut them into thin slices. Tossing them in a mixture of flour, sugar and cinnamon, they were ready to be put into the pie plate. She covered it with the remaining dough and cut vents in the top after brushing it with an egg wash. It was Grayson's favorite meal and she was praying that it would lift his spirits. She called her mother then to finalize the drop off plans for Labor Day. On speaker phone, Chloe's voice was lively as she told her mother all about the fun activities they did. And she bragged about the yummy food that she would be bringing home to share with the family. Arabella smiled to herself after the call. Her daughter's special bond with her Gran was heartwarming.

"Mom, this smells heavenly. I cannot wait to eat, I'm starving?" Ariana walked into the kitchen and lifted the lids to peer inside each pot. Do you want my help with anything?"

"Sure, will you set the table for us please?" Opening the oven door, she removed the roast to rest as she mashed the potatoes with a splash of cream and butter. Grayson came in as she was putting everything in bowls for them to help themselves. She brought over the roast on a serving dish and placed it in front of Grayson to carve.

"Delicious, what a feast you've prepared for us! Thank you, Arabella." He smiled happily at her and she saw a glimpse of the old Grayson. Her heart felt warm and fuzzy.

"You're welcome, I love doing it for you." She passed the bowls around to Ariana as Grayson began to carve the meat. His tremors began as soon as he started and after a few uneven slices, he dropped the utensils in a fury.

"I'm not hungry!" Throwing the chair back, he stood up unsteadily and stormed out of the dining room with Arabella following him.

"Grayson, it's okay. I'll help you, please allow me to support you." Tears sprang to her eyes as he put on his shoes to leave. He looked passed her with hardened eyes as she pleaded with him. "Where are you going?"

"I want to go out for a bit, to clear my head. I'll be back in a while." Before she could argue further, he got into his car, opened the garage door and then backed down the laneway in a fury. She went back to join Ariana for dinner, but she didn't feel like eating now. Her stomach was upset and she wanted to cry.

"Where's dad? Isn't he eating with us?" The concern was evident on her face and she was worried for her family.

"No, honey. He just needed to take some time for himself. Hopefully, when he comes back, he'll see just how much we love and care for him." She pretended to pick at her food hoping that Ariana didn't notice. Afterwards, she served the apple pie that she made warm with a big scoop of ice cream.

"Mom, you are really the best cook. This is so good!" Her blue eyes sparkled like her fathers and she missed him being there. She smiled at her daughter now fifteen. How quickly time flies, she thought. Chloe was thirteen and beginning high school in just a couple of days as well. Both of her girls were growing up so fast. They cleared the plates and loaded the dishwasher chatting about the back-to-school outfits that Ariana couldn't decide on. Then, after grabbing the cashmere throw, they got cozy on the sofa to watch a movie with Simon their cat. After it was finished, Arabella glanced at the time noticing that it was after ten o'clock.

"I wonder where dad is mom? It's getting late." She had changed into her pajamas and sat nestled against her mother as they watched more television. Her hand reached out to caress Simon's soft fur.

"I don't know. This certainly isn't like him. I am going to try calling him." As it rang, she could hear the reverberation of the sound echoing somewhere in her house. She walked cautiously upstairs and noticed his cellphone on the vanity in the washroom. He had left it at home; there was no way to reach him. She went back downstairs to sit with her daughter feeling disturbingly unsettled. Like she was underwater and couldn't breathe properly.

Meanwhile, Grayson was at the veterinary clinic drowning his sorrows in a bottle of scotch. He just wanted his health back, to be able to operate again and be carefree like his younger days. Sitting at his desk with his hands on his head in self pity drinking, he sipped it straight from the bottle. Years ago, he would have found the taste much too bitter to drink without some sort of a mix, but he developed a liking to it now. Nasty, like he was feeling inside. He passed out a few times, before falling into a slumber snoring softly. Startled, Grayson woke a short time later, feeling groggy and slightly unwell. He stood up wobbly reaching for the keys on his desk, then drove down the road swerving in and out of the oncoming lanes. Luckily, it was late so the roads were clear of other cars.

He reached home without incident and pressed the garage door opener on his rearview mirror with an unsteady hand. Once inside, he pushed it again and the door closed down with a soft humming sound. He almost fell down getting out of the car and staggered up to the mud room door, eyes glazed. As he opened it, one of his shoes came off so he removed the other before realizing that he left the car running. He sauntered back and pulled open the door hastily, climbing into the seat to turn it off. Instead, he pulled his hand back, mesmerized by the song playing on the radio. It was his and Arabella's favorite one, almost like it was written for them. The ballad that they held hands to skating for the first time together. She had tricked him into believing that she couldn't skate at all and then performed an incredible dance routine. A vision of loveliness, an angel, all dressed in white with skin like a porcelain doll. He remembered her beauty and poise as she twirled around the ice like a princess. Arabella stole his heart that day and he knew that he loved her then. They also chose that very song for their wedding dance; it was one of the happiest days of his life. Including when each of their daughters were born. He smiled peacefully and laid his head back on the headrest recollecting those glorious moments as warm tears slid down his cheeks. His precious Arabella, the love of his life.

It was to those memories that Grayson passed out and never woke up. Both Ariana and Arabella were asleep on the sofa in the other room and didn't hear him come home. His shoes had become stuck in the door to the house, allowing the toxic fumes to overtake them. Neither woke up, succumbing to lethal carbon monoxide poisoning as well.

Meanwhile that morning in Sarnia, Chloe helped her Gran load up the trunk with all of the goodies that they had prepared and they were on their way. There was a soft rain, barely enough to wet the ground as they drove down the highway chatting happily. By the time that they reached London, the sun had made a welcome appearance. She pulled into a vacant parking spot at the restaurant and she and Chloe walked Coco on the grass. It was one of the few places to eat that were open on

Labor Day and they were shown to a table on the patio within minutes. Coco was well behaved and laid down beside them. While poring over the menus, the server brought them glasses of ice water.

"Welcome, my name is Kate! Can I bring you anything other than the water for now?" She was extremely pleasant and carried a little notepad in her apron.

"May I have a hot chocolate please? Plenty of whip cream!" Chloe made sure that she accentuated that part. Even though the day was warm, she still enjoyed it.

"Of course, darling. Anything for you ma'am?"

"A pot of Earl Gray tea please with milk and honey." Layla continued to mull over the extensive menu and decided on the Eggs Benedict. But they would wait to put in their order until Arabella, Grayson and Ariana joined them. She glanced at her watch thinking that they would be there shortly. Kate brought their beverages with extra whip cream for Chloe and told them she would be back when the others arrived. She sipped her tea patiently and watched her granddaughter enjoy her hot chocolate noticing that it was getting late. There were two other tables also sitting outside eating.

"I'm getting so hungry Gran. When can we put in our order?" There was a small whip cream mustache above her lip.

"I don't know what's keeping them. I'm going to call now and see." Arabella's cellphone rang and rang, before going to voicemail. Layla left a short message and then called Grayson's, only to find the same outcome. Puzzled, she called Ariana on hers and received no answer either. All three calls going to voicemail? She knew that Ariana was always on her phone and couldn't understand what was happening.

Chloe's tummy was growling. "Are they coming soon Gran?"

"I'm sure that they will be here any moment. Why don't we place our orders and start without them." Her stomach was in knots and she couldn't shake the eerie sensation that haunted her to the very core. The only other time she had ever had that feeling was when she was carrying her second child, Lincoln. She recalled how he had suddenly stopped kicking inside of her and how fear crept into her thoughts. They were over an hour late without any notice, nor could she reach them. She motioned to the server and she hurried over with her notepad and pen ready.

"We would like to put in our order and hopefully it won't be much longer for the additional parties. Chloe, go ahead dear."

"I would like the pancakes and crispy bacon please. And a glass of orange juice."

Layla didn't feel like eating; her appetite lost with the worry that engulfed her. "The Eggs Benedict sounds nice for me, thank you." She handed back hers and Chloe's menus, but Kate left the other three on the table. She then stood up to look for them in the parking lot. There was no sign of Grayson's SUV. The day was bright and sunny, so the visibility was clear. She tried calling each again to receive the same results and went back to sit with Chloe. The food arrived shortly after that, but she just picked at it praying for her daughter and family to be safe. Kate was sweet and brought over an ice cream sundae for Chloe with chocolate sauce and more whipped cream. It only distressed her more as she remembered Arabella's love for chocolate or choclate as she used to call it.

Finally, she couldn't cope with her racing thoughts anymore and called the police. She had excused herself from her granddaughter so she wouldn't alarm her and stood inside the front entrance. At first, they just thought that she was fretting for nothing. An overly worried grandma. But as they listened more to her worries, they believed that it was worth looking into.

"We want you to go back home and wait until you receive further information, Ms. Dawson."

"But, shouldn't I go to my daughter's home in Oakville?" She needed to find out what was going on.

"No, please do as instructed until further notice. We will be in touch." They hung up and she did as she was told by the officer.

"Come now, we will return to Sarnia until we hear more." Layla choked out the words.

Chloe looked shocked. "But, why are we going back to your place Gran? Where's mom and dad? And Ariana?" Layla hugged her trying to remain brave for her sake. Her heart couldn't take anymore pain; she just couldn't bear it. She said a prayer in her head.

"Come, let's drive and we'll talk more." Instead of speaking in the car, both were subdued the whole way back to Sarnia while Coco rested. The sky had become gray again with dark clouds and looked ominous.

It was just before six o'clock that their lives would change forever. A police car pulled up into Layla's driveway and the officer got out slowly. He hated this type of work, dreading it more than anything. When the report came in, he had felt sick. Almost an entire family perishing and now he had to tell the remaining family members. The Oakville police as well as the fire trucks had followed up on Layla's concerns and arrived at their home to find the gruesome discovery. The car was still idling in the garage so they donned protective equipment and breathing apparatus's before entering. They left the garage door open to clear the fumes out as they pulled Grayson from the car. He had no vital signs and was determined deceased on the spot.

Inside they found Arabella hugging Ariana as if they were still sleeping on the sofa from the night before. Simon, their Siamese cat curled up beside them, also overcome by the carbon monoxide poisoning. It was such a tragedy and totally preventable. Grayson hadn't been keeping up with replacing the batteries in the detectors and his careless drinking had cost all of them their lives. Some of the neighbors had gathered on the street when they noticed all of the emergency vehicles. The police investigated more while waiting for the coroner to arrive to remove all of the bodies. Autopsies would also be issued to accurately determine the cause of each of the deaths.

Officer Bains closed the cruiser door firmly and locked it. He removed his hat, took a deep breath and pressed the doorbell.

Layla looked out of her window and gasped when she saw the police car in her driveway. "Officer, what is it?" She clutched her throat unable to get air as she invited him in. Chloe was out walking Coco around the neighborhood. They stood inside the front door as he spoke.

"My name is Officer Bains and I have some terrible news to deliver. Shall we sit down for a moment?"

"No, please just tell me what has happened." Her voice sounded hoarse, almost insolent."

"There has been an accident which regrettably has taken the lives of your daughter Arabella, her husband Grayson and your granddaughter Ariana Burke."

Layla felt dizziness and clutched the wall for support. He took her arm and guided her to the soft velvet settee in the sitting room where she broke down in sobs.

"No, this can't be true. Please tell me that they're fine." Her words were muffled by her hands covering her mouth in horror.

He sincerely wished that he could. "I'm deeply sorry for your substantial loss."

"How, how did this happen? Was it a car accident?" Layla was hyperventilating.

He gulped before answering. "It was carbon monoxide poisoning. All succumbed to the toxic fumes." He went on to tell her as much as he was able to as she looked at him withered similar to a dying plant.

"Grayson left the car running in the garage? Why would he do that?"

"It would appear that he was under the influence of alcohol so we are treating it like an accidental poisoning at this point. Of course, more investigation is needed."

Layla was filled with mixed emotions digesting each piece of information like a buffet dinner, except she wasn't relishing it at all. Feeling angry hearing that it was Grayson's carelessness that caused all of their deaths, she lowered her head into her hands.

"I wanted to give you this. It contains the valuables that each was wearing at the time of death." He handed it to her with great remorse as she took it and held it against her chest for dear life. There was a delicate knocking on the front door, almost inaudible then. Officer Bains went to open it while Layla wept tears of devastation. She felt a hopelessness wash over her that she had never felt before.

It was Anna at the door, looking deeply concerned for her neighbor and friend, offering her help.

"Layla, are you okay? Do you need me to come inside?" They both shared the loss of a husband and they had become even closer friends after that.

"Yes, please allow her to come in officer." Anna ran to her and hugged her knowing that something tragic had happened. The officer left shortly after that promising to be in contact soon with details on how to proceed with the burial plans. He was shaken up as he sat in his cruiser, feeling sad for the grandmother and her grandchild. They sat together on the settee as Layla explained what had happened and Anna was devastated for them.

"I'm so sorry Layla. How horrible! This is just so life shattering." It was quite a shock and so very tragic. Chloe came home at that moment with Coco and they both ran into the living room, out of breath.

"Gran, what's happened, is everything all right?" She noticed their tears and immediately began crying as well.

"Come here sweetheart." She reached for her and Anna went to the kitchen to prepare some tea, allowing them to talk in private. Layla took a deep breath and began to tell her what had happened, praying for the strength not to break down. If it wasn't for Chloe, she would have lost all will to live now.

Chloe screamed like there were two hands around her neck strangling her, squeezing the air from her lungs. Layla wished that she could take her agony away, but she had never felt so helpless in her life. She prayed to God to help them overcome the biggest obstacle in their lives.

"Why does God keep taking everyone that we love Gran? It's not fair." Her sobs enveloped each word smothering them until she couldn't talk anymore. She rested her head on Layla's lap and Anna approached cautiously with a tray, setting it down on the coffee table. There were cookies and squares as well, but it was a formality as she knew neither would eat any of them.

"Thank you, that is so nice of you." Layla watched as she poured the tea from the pot into a delicate matching Royal Albert teacup. Dainty with small flowers, the set was gifted to her and Winston on their wedding day by her mother Annette. Such a day of joy then, not nightmarish like now. Chloe raised her head slowly and sat up. Her chestnut hair was matted by the salty tears to the side of her cheek. Anna handed it to her and poured some for Chloe. But she shook her head "*no*". Layla brought it to her lips, but tasted nothing as she swallowed the hot liquid. Nothing but a bitter aftertaste that had nothing to do with the tea.

Later when Chloe was resting, Layla sat hesitantly on her bed staring at the bag that the police officer had given her before he left. She could see that it held Grayson's watch as well as their wedding rings as she opened it with nimble fingers. Holding the bag upside down, she allowed the contents to spill out onto her duvet. Her mind tried not to think about where they were now as she stared at the very possessions that touched their bodies last.

Arabella's locket twinkled as she picked it up, squeezing more anguish into her body as she remembered her always wearing it. Layla wiped her eyes, blew her nose and then opened it revealing the three photographs inside. Grayson, wearing an appealing smile was first and she removed it furiously, wanting to rip it into a million pieces. But, she didn't. When her heart stopped beating erratically to a slower pace, she carefully removed her sweet Chloe's photograph and placed it into her jewelry box. Then, she looked through the most recent photographs that she took of Arabella and chose one for the first frame. As she cut out the small oval picture, she was flooded by memories of so many beautiful times gone by. Never would she or Chloe be blessed with them again. After which she put Grayson's in the middle, followed by Ariana's who stunning smile was warm and captivating like her fathers. Before he began his excessive drinking.

They both seemed to swim underwater for the next few days that followed. Chloe stayed home with Gran to mourn her loss instead of starting high school as she normally would have.

"Gran, I miss them so much. The pain is worse than anything I've ever known in my life. Even when Grandpa died." Her face was drawn as she spoke.

"You're older now and you understand the meaning of death and losing loved ones further. This is something that no young lady should ever have to deal with. But you never know what you'll encounter in life. Good or bad, just know that you must navigate through it in the best way that you can."

On Sunday morning, Layla prepared a breakfast of scrambled eggs and bacon for them. Neither had their appetites back fully, but she wanted to make something hearty before church. She was wearing a black dress along with a pearl necklace which graced her delicate neck. Chloe came down in her pajamas, yawning and looking very unhappy. Her face was angry as she sat in her chair with her eyebrows creased frowning.

"Why aren't you dressed? Church will begin soon." She placed her plate in front of her.

Chloe pouted. "I'm not going Gran. I'm mad at him for taking my family to heaven. And grandpa. Lincoln too, even though I wasn't born back then."

Layla's face softened. "I understand dear and that's alright. You don't have to attend with me. Try to eat something though." They picked at their breakfast and Chloe rushed upstairs as she was tidying up. She came down just as Layla was putting on her comfortable black shoes in a black and white floral dress. It was demure, but lovely with ruffles at the hem. A small gold clip held her chestnut hair back from her beautiful, but desolate face.

"I've changed my mind Gran. I would like to come with you." She sighed, like it was being forced out of her body.

"Thank you, Chloe. I have something that I know you will treasure. May I put it on for you?" She held it up for her to see and unfastened it.

Overwhelmed with sorrow, she nodded. Lifting the familiar locket with both hands, she opened it slowly knowing very well what it held inside.

She wrapped her arms around her. "You're all that I have left now Gran. I love you so much." She mourned for her parents and sister; never to hear their voices again. They drove the short distance to the church, each deep in thought and not looking forward the days to come. Many of the congregation offered their condolences and Anna sat with them through the service. The pastor asked everyone pray for them during their difficult times and preached in great lengths about the healing process.

"Blessed are those who mourn, for they shall be comforted." His words touched Chloe and her Gran as he went on to tell a story about a devastating loss that he experienced years ago. After they sang hymns, they walked to the large wooden doors to leave. Pastor Luke shook their hands warmly as Layla thanked him for his touching service.

Planning all three funerals was unfathomable to Layla and with the help of Anna she foraged through it. Not without heartache and bottomless tears, though. They were to be buried in Sarnia with the other members of the family in the same cemetery as their wills stated. Layla planned a committal service for immediate family and close friends only. Grayson and Arabella's close neighbors were invited along with the staff at both clinics where they worked. It would be private and intimate without a reception afterwards. Chloe began high school reluctantly, because Layla did not wish for her to be involved in the morbid planning of it all. She chose two shiny cherry wood caskets for Arabella as well as Grayson and one white one for Ariana. White was the symbol of purity as the funeral planner told her. After she was finished choosing, she went into the washroom and threw up into the toilet hoping to dissipate the agony that gripped her body mercilessly. The bile that she felt continuously in the back of her throat was a constant reminder of the pain and anguish that overtook her.

The day of the funeral was unrighteously sunny and gloriously warm for a September day. Deep down, Layla had wished for rain, tears from heaven, but they didn't listen. Anna drove her and Chloe to the cemetery, driving slowly behind the black hearses with their car lights on. All three were parked behind each other blatantly flaunting devastation and heartbreak for the surviving loved ones. Each casket was painstakingly removed and carried by the pallbearers to the grave site while they watched in agony. White folding chairs were set up in neat rows in front of the three caskets which were a pathetic sight. Each one was closed and not open, she couldn't bear it, her heart would stop beating to see them lifeless. Doc Benson, his wife Marie as well as Glenda and her husband were the first to arrive, paying their respect to each of the deceased before taking a seat in the second row. Some of their close neighbors from Oakville who drove down to Sarnia together, were seated after paying their respects. The staff from Grayson's clinic arrived and stood crying together over the catastrophic loss. Dr. Michael, Grayson's associate took Layla's hand offering his condolences. All attendees were given a service program with a lovely tribute honoring each of them and a special poem written by Chloe. As she sat in the front row with her face buried in the shoulder of Gran's black dress, she heard a familiar voice.

She turned to look, the sunshine was blinding and it nipped at her swollen eyes, similar to multiple bee stings. Silently, she wished that she was blind so she wouldn't have to see the pain on top of feeling it.

"Hi Chloe. I just wanted to say that I'm so sorry about what happened. It's really sad. This is for you." Oliver, wearing a black suit with a tie, handed her a small wooden box that she remembered very well and knew what was inside.

She was hesitant, but reached for it gingerly. Intricately carved with vines, she opened it finding the three treasured sand dollars inside that she had always admired.

Gasping she asked. "Oliver, are you sure?" She didn't know if she should accept it from him, he treasured it greatly.

Nodding yes, he said. "I want you to have them now." He went back to sit with his parents Hannah and Owen beside his younger sister Hope. The other neighbors were seated near them looking mournful in silence. Pastor Luke began the service shortly after.

"Today we are gathered together at this graveside service for three precious loved ones who lost their lives tragically and much too soon. On behalf of the family, I would like to thank all of you for coming today." He paused for a bit, dabbing his eyes and continued with a sentimental prayer before inviting Layla up to deliver the eulogy. As she rose, Chloe stood up and took her hand walking with her to offer support.

Layla held Winston's handkerchief tightly in her hand as she spoke tenderly about her daughter first, then Ariana next. Her voice caught on a sob when she spoke Grayson's name and she couldn't continue. Overcome with grief, she cried while Chloe stood beside her helplessly. Then, Chloe began to speak softly reciting her poem that she wrote while Layla smiled at her through her tears. After that, she walked over with the precious carved box and opening it, took out a sand dollar and placed it on her mother's casket. Next, she laid one on top of her father's and the last one for her sister Ariana. Gently, she closed the box crying for the family she lost and questioning everything in her life now. Layla held out her arms and Chloe raced into them, thankful that she still had her Gran. After she sat down in her seat, she looked back at Oliver hoping that he wasn't angry with her for parting with the sand dollars. Tears ran down his cheeks as he smiled and nodded his approval as the other guests cried openly.

The pastor closed the ceremony with a prayer that touched Layla's heart and then it was over. She felt even worse, knowing that after they left each casket would be lowered solemnly into the ground. The headstones would then be positioned on top. The double heart one in marble for Arabella and Grayson to share. And Ariana's with a dog on it to signify her love of animals. Left to rest there forever through each of the four seasons with her other loved ones. The guests approached them one by one to say goodbye. Layla clung to them for dear life as Chloe watched in a trance.

"We're so sorry for your loss, such a terrible tragedy. The office just isn't the same without her." Doc Benson cried openly as his wife consoled him.

"Thank you for coming." As he walked away, Chloe ran after him.

"Doc Benson, what are you going to do with my mom's office?" Caught off guard, he answered honestly. "I haven't thought about that. I don't want to do anything right now with it. Why do you ask?"

"I decided just a few weeks ago that I want to become an optometrist like my mother. I was going to tell her when I got back from visiting with my Gran, but now it's too late. She will never know my wish to follow in her footsteps." Chloe cried openly and he hugged her sympathetically.

"I will make you a promise then. Her office is yours if you want it. I won't touch a thing."

"But it will take years for me to get a degree in optometry!" She looked astonished.

"Then, it will wait for you!" Chloe hugged him again before he left. Oliver came over to talk with her next.

"I hope that you're not upset about the sand dollars."

"Not at all. I think that what you did was heroic and unselfish." He smiled at her.

She handed him the empty box but he wouldn't take it.

"You keep it. One day you'll fill it again with more sand dollars, I promise."

"Thanks Oliver." They said their goodbyes and after everyone was gone, Anna drove them back home. Later that evening, Layla and Chloe walked over to their favorite chip truck and sat together on a bench facing the water. Both munched slowly on the fries in silence, not really feeling like eating.

It took several weeks before Layla was brave enough to clean out the house in Oakville. Anna helped her as well as several of the neighbors, but it still wrenched her heart. Chloe and Coco stayed back in Sarnia with one of her girlfriends and would spend the night there. Layla thought it would be best that way, especially knowing how hard it would be to go through the personal items. Just being there was heartbreaking, the happy memories flooding her mind. Then the trauma of their deaths eating at her soul. The keepsakes were put into storage for Chloe and then the house was listed for sale furnished. Surprisingly, even after the bad aura associated with it, the home sold fairly quickly. Layla put all of the proceeds from the sale in a trust fund for her.

Chapter 11

Chloe's convocation reminded Layla of her precious Arabella's so many years ago. Through the veil of fresh tears, she saw her sweet daughter walking across the stage in her gown and cap to collect her diploma. Turning with it in her hands, she had waved happily to her mother in the crowd. As Layla blinked, the warm tears were released slowly from her eyes, casting a more defined view. Smiling, she waved back at Chloe as Doc Benson and the others from the optometry office clapped vigorously. She was a vision of Arabella with her chestnut hair and red lips. Now Dr. Chloe Burke and they couldn't be prouder! She was living permanently in Oakville just a stone's throw from her mother's office, which was now hers. Doc Benson had kept his promise after so many years and it was exactly as she had left it. Chloe worked through the summers to train alongside him and was happiest when caring for the patients. The first time that she walked into her mother's office, an overwhelming grief devoured her body and she mourned all of her losses. Her hand, like a soft whisper, caressed the desk recalling the day her she purchased it in Toronto. The sheer delight that it eluded when her father had agreed to purchase it. And how she and Ariana browsed together in the exquisite shop, never thinking that it wouldn't always be that way. Happy and carefree.

Chloe sat for a long time in her mother's chair, trying hard to digest the pain. It was heartbreaking and for a moment she wondered if she had made a mistake coming back to it. Pulling a bunch of tissue from the box, she covered her eyes with them and cried freely. Recalling the paintings, she turned around in the chair to gaze at them on the wall. Her mother believed that they resembled Chloe and Ariana, falling in love with them upon first sight. A small crystal frame sat on the corner of the desk and Chloe picked it up reminiscing. It was a family photograph taken just weeks before it happened. Coco, their adored dog was even in the picture and new tears began. She had passed away shortly after Chloe had left for university and once more it was another blow. The family dog was special to her. Oh, how she wished she could go back to that point in time again and halt it. Similar to an old antique clock without a key to wind it, stifled in that point of time eternally.

Glenda knocked on her door. "Welcome Chloe, I just wanted to see if there is anything that I can do for you? We're going to love having you here for the summer." Chloe's flushed face and swollen eyes told her how difficult it was for her.

"That's nice, but no thank you. I can't believe the emotions that I'm feeling right now. I miss her so much, my dad and sister also. I knew that this would be difficult coming back, but this is a real punch in the stomach."

"I understand honey. No one expects for you to be brave all the time. If it's any consolation, I know that they would all be especially proud of you. You're going to be great." Her face showed limitless empathy.

Chloe smiled. "Yes, I appreciate that, Glenda." They spoke for a bit longer before she went back to work at the front desk. Chloe settled in nicely over time and loved working with Doc Benson. She loved his charismatic personality and his funny jokes. They reminded her of her fathers.

Now, she was finally an optometrist, Dr. Chloe Burke! She was subdued as she unpacked some personal items that she had brought in from her condo. All very sentimental to her heart. Lifting the small wooden box out first, she closed her eyes and made a wish before she opened it. Praying that the three sand dollars would still be inside. But regretfully, it only revealed the same emptiness that she now felt in her heart and she snapped it shut. It made her think about that painful day of the funeral when Oliver gave it to her filled with the intricate items. Solemnly, she set it on one of the shelves on the grand bookcase and stepped away from it. There was also the porcelain vase that her mother prised and she placed it on a round table in front of the window. Butterflies were meticulously painted on it as were the tiny sprays of flowers. Chloe always adored the eye-catching arrangements that her mother placed in it. She made a mental note to purchase a bouquet of flowers to compliment it. Sighing wistfully, she then went to tend to her patients, thus taking her mind off of the ill fate that now haunted her life.

Gran had helped her purchase the two-bedroom condo on the fourth floor with a view of the lake with the inheritance of her parents. It was airy and modern, yet it didn't compromise charm with its high ceilings and open elegant design. Fully equipped with all the amenities one could dream of, including a swimming pool, exercise room and roof top garden. The serene outdoor space was peaceful and would provide relaxation for Chloe after work. There were tranquil views from each of the spacious rooms and a kitchen that one could only dream about. Layla felt as though another piece of her heart was lost when she left for university several years back. Chloe came back home to Sarnia for the first few summers and holidays before transitioning into her work with Doc Benson. The enduring move to take over her mother's place at the optometry office left her feeling isolated. All of it reminded her of when

A Gran Scheme

Arabella left for school and then Oakville with Grayson to begin her career. Except, she had Winston then. Now she was alone, but she tried to make the best of it. Chloe invited her to stay as frequently as she desired and her good friend and neighbor Anna was a godsend. Both were members of the local senior's centre enjoying all of the activities that were offered to fill their time.

After a brief period of condo living, Chloe sought more space and a yard of her own, so she hired a real agent to help. That's when she had found her forever home that made her feel happy and at peace. It would have been her dream for her Gran to move in, but she wouldn't hear of it. She felt that Chloe was young and deserved to have her private life without an old lady imposing. But Chloe didn't feel that way, she loved her so much. The truth was that her Gran didn't want to leave all of her loved ones that were at rest there. She visited them weekly, sometimes sitting for hours on a picnic blanket that she would place on the grass in front of their headstones. Even on the inclement days, she would bundle up and go to be close to them. A harmony radiated deep within her as she spoke tenderly to each of them. The burden that she carried each day was only evident to her, no one would have guessed the weight of it. She was kind to people and always offered her help whenever she was able.

When Anna was diagnosed with cancer, her only son Felix who was a medical doctor abroad in Sweden, hired live-in help to assist. Layla also visited with her for long periods daily, playing cards and reading to her. June, the registered nurse and her husband Carl who was a personal support worker were a true blessing. They cooked, cleaned and cared for Anna until she became incapacitated with pain. She was unable to eat or keep anything in her stomach and was experiencing bouts of confusion. Layla was puzzled as to why Felix didn't come down even once to visit his sickly mother who didn't have much time to live. June and Carl seemed to brush off her questions about Anna's son with excuses about his work. As a doctor who also volunteered his time in third world countries, they told her that he was unable to fly back. Christmas came and passed and in early February, June knocked on her door.

"Hi, please come in. How is Anna? Is everything alright?" Layla invited her into the kitchen and put the kettle on to make tea for them.

"No, regrettably Anna's son has made the difficult decision to place her in a Hospice. I wanted to tell you because I know how close you both are." June looked unhappy, her mouth grim.

"Oh, dear. I am sorry to hear that. How soon will she be moved there?" The high-pitched sound of the kettle interrupted their conversation and Layla stood up quickly. She poured the boiling water into the tea pot and placed cream and sugar on the tray, bringing it to the table. A plate of freshly baked snickerdoodle cookies was added as she sat down to pour the tea into the delicate cups.

"Thank you for the tea. She'll be going in just a couple of days to a Hospice in London, Ontario that specializes in quality end-of-life treatment." June took a gulp from the tea cup and reached for a warm cookie. Her hair looked unkempt and her face was void of any makeup. Black horned rimmed glasses framed her small, beady eyes as she devoured it hungrily, not caring if she made a mess.

"London? I would have hoped that Anna would have been placed somewhere locally here in Sarnia so that I could visit often." Her disappointment was evident as she wrung her hands anxiously, wanting to break down and cry.

June reached over for another cookie, taking a huge bite, causing crumbs to fall onto her baggy sweatshirt and pants. She seemed not to notice or care perhaps as she swallowed another gulp of tea to wash it down.

"Well, neither Carl or I had any say at all. We were taking such good care of her too. Her son has asked us to stay on and house sit though so we'll be here for you if you need anything." Layla watched as she took her arm and swiped at her mouth with her sleeve. Then, she stood up and Layla walked her to the front door still reeling from the news. She paused for a moment before opening the door and spoke softly.

"Do you mind if I come over to visit her tomorrow? I'd like to spend as much time as I can with her before she leaves."

"Of course not. And I'll also let you know what time the patient transfer service is coming so you can say your goodbyes as well." Layla watched her as she waddled over her front lawn to Anna's house next door. She remembered something Chloe said to her and it resonated inside of her. *"Why does God keep taking everyone that we love Gran? It's not fair."* She said a prayer then, hoping that it would give her strength. Knowing that her good friend was dying of cancer was agonising. June and Carl kept Layla informed of Anna's condition and even offered to take her to London to visit. They seemed to be always there probing her and she didn't know whether to be grateful or concerned.

Layla called Chloe shortly afterwards as she was eager to speak with her granddaughter.

"Hi, I miss you so much! You look wonderful dear." Layla wanted to kiss the tablet; she was so happy to see her. Even if it wasn't in person.

Chloe noticed the intense strain on her face. "Gran, I miss you as well! I'm so sorry that Anna's health is failing. How are you coping?"

"Not good. They are moving her to a Hospice in London so she won't be close to me anymore. I truly don't know why Felix chose one so far away."

"Oh, no Gran, that's so sad! There are good ones there in Sarnia for her, surely." Chloe knew just how close they both had become, it was a shame.

"Yes, I believe there are. The couple who has been caring for her will continue to live in her home. They seem to be very helpful and have even offered to drive me to visit Anna in London once she is settled."

"That's really kind of them Gran. Why don't I take a couple of days off of work to come down?" Chloe was concerned for her now that her close friend would be leaving.

"Oh, no please don't do that Chloe. You're so busy and I'll be alright."

Chloe knew that she wouldn't want to inconvenience her. "You're the most important to me Gran. Will you promise to call me if you need anything?"

"Of course I will. I love you so much."

"I love you Gran. Talk soon." Chloe felt worried as she hung up. She sat for a moment on the sofa gazing at the hardwood floors that were installed several months ago. They looked beautiful and the color was immaculate, praising the furnishings that she had meticulously chosen. The exotic natural walnut was also made in Canada. She was worried for her Gran, wondering how she would cope without her best friend Anna. But Chloe knew how solid she was and that she would try to make the best of things. It was from her that she had learned so much. That of strength and resilience. Fortunately, Gran stayed active and involved in daily activities at the local senior's centre despite her despair.

On the day of Anna's move to London, Layla sat with her on the bed holding her delicate hand. She tried to be brave for her friend's sake, but she was feeling dreadful. Anna was drifting in and out of a tranquilness due to the medication that she was given intravenously. Frequently, Layla could feel her squeeze her hand gently as she struggled for each breath. Her frail body was covered with several blankets even though the house was especially warm. Anna had lost so much weight over the last few months; cancer was a terrible disease. But she still smiled at Layla when she opened her eyes for a short period of time. The room was quiet except for a small brass clock on her bedside table which ticked at sharp, even intervals. Layla wished that she could hush the imminent sound that was counting down the moments of what laid ahead for her dear friend.

June came briskly into the room. "They have arrived. It's time for Anna to go." She disconnected the IV from the pole and began to roll back the blankets as Carl brought in the attendants. There were two males in uniform pushing a stretcher which they carefully lifted her onto, then fastened the straps. June covered her up again to keep her warm. Layla smoothed back her hair and gave her a kiss on the forehead. She forced herself to step back with her heart in her throat. They laid the intravenous bag on top of the blanket as they wheeled her outside and into the patient transfer vehicle.

June hugged Layla as it drove away taking a small part of her heart with it. "This is hard for you, I know. Can we do anything for you?"

"No, thank you though. I am going to go home to rest for now." Laying in bed, she stared at the ceiling feeling lonely knowing that things were always changing. She detested change even though it was inevitable. After a short period, she got up to change to go swimming at the recreation centre. It always gave her a boost of liveliness to see some of her friends and she knew that they would want to hear about Anna.

After she swam, Layla stopped off at the library to collect some interesting books to read. She found some murder mystery novels by a new author that promised to be thrilling. Whenever she visited, it reminded her of Winston and how they had met so many years ago now. His desk was long since gone, but she remembered exactly where it used to be with the jar of sweets on top. Now, everything was modernized with computers and scanners for people to check out the books. Back home, she popped a chicken pot pie in the oven to have with a tossed salad which she prepared. As she diced the ripe, red tomatoes and cucumber into nice even slices, her tablet rang. Delighted, she saw that it was Chloe and quickly wiped her hands on a tea towel before answering. "Hello Chloe, it's so nice of you to call!"

"Hi Gran. How are you holding up? Today was the day that Anna was moving and I was worried about you." She felt heartbroken for Anna, she had become part of their family.

"Yes, dear. It was truly devastating. I know that it would have been her wish to live out her last days in her home. Now, she will be in a place where she knows no one. In a strange city without friends or family."

"That's sad. We can make plans to visit her soon Gran. I will take you."

Gran smiled causing the fine lines on her face to deepen. She looked unusually pale in the kitchen light which casted a soft glow as the November sky darkened.

"Thank you, Chloe, I appreciate that. How is work? I bet that you're so busy with your days now."

"Yes, it is busy. But I love my work. Caring for some of mom's patients and hearing them tell stories about her. They all loved her so much Gran." She began to cry openly.

"I know sweetheart, she was a blessing to everyone who knew her. She is missed by many." Gran's eyes were moist as she spoke and she yearned to take her granddaughter into her arms.

"I miss all of them so much! There are always so many reminders here, everywhere I look, I feel her presence. I drove by our old home the other day Gran and it was agonizing." Sobbing, Chloe wiped her eyes with a handful of tissues.

Gran sighed deeply. "It must have been very difficult to do that Chloe. Are you okay?"

"Yes, I don't feel the need to do it again, but I was curious. Almost expecting dad to be out front mowing the lawn and mom gardening contentedly. So, wanting to catch a glimpse of Ariana riding her bicycle down the street or laughing with her friends. Instead, I saw the new family enjoying while mine was brutally taken away. They even smiled and waved at me. The garage door was open and I had to drive away."

"I can't imagine how you felt. But I do know that we have each other to lean on." She smiled.

"Always Gran. I love you so much. Let me know when you would like to visit Anna okay?"

"I will. Take care and I adore you sweet granddaughter." Layla sat for a moment mesmerized by the things that Chloe had said. She remembered when she walked into the home for the first time after the accident. The spine-tingling grip that siphoned the air from her lungs promising no recourse. She stopped herself then, not wanting to rework any of the dark moments in her mind. Standing up, she finished the salad and took out her piping hot pot pie. Not feeling very hungry she picked slowly at the dinner she prepared feeling isolated. Afterwards, she chose one of the books from the library and settled comfortably in her reclining chair to read.

The doorbell rang the next morning as she was tidying her home. She peered cautiously through the small glass window and saw June standing there. She opened the door and invited her in.

"Hi Layla. I wanted to pop over and make sure that you are okay. It was terrible watching Anna leave yesterday. It must have been very difficult for you." She touched her arm and smiled causing her eyes to become mere slits behind her glasses. Her hair hadn't seen a brush for days.

"I'm managing, thank you. I just hope that we can visit her soon."

June nodded happily. "Yes, Carl and I are planning to go tomorrow if you'd like to join us?"

"I would love to go with you to see Anna. What time?" Layla's heart was beating fast like a drum.

"Would 9:00 a.m. work for you? That way we can spend the day and go out to lunch in between."

"Yes, that would be fine! I'll be ready to go." Layla and June exchanged cell numbers as well so that they could call each other. Layla went out then to run some errands.

She awoke early the next morning excited to spend time with her poor friend. She patted a light moisturizer on her face and put a dab of lipstick on her lips. After arranging her hair in a flattering style, she dressed in a cream cowl neck sweater and brown dress pants. She sat eagerly in her kitchen sipping the last of her tea leaving a faint lipstick mark on the edge as she watched the clock. At five minutes to nine, she put on her comfortable boots and a camel-colored wool coat. In her large tote bag, she placed her wallet along with her keys, some snacks and a book of poetry that she chose from the library to read to Anna. The poems were beautiful as well as inspirational and she hoped that they would sooth her. Lastly, there was a lovely floral arrangement that the local florist Marabel made up for her. She knew Layla well and the heartbreak that she went through over the years and had also supplied the flowers to her then. This time she chose brightly-coloured roses, gerbera daisies, commercial mums, lilies and cymbidium orchids for the cheerful display. June tapped on her door shortly after and carried the floral box for her as she locked up. Layla followed her to the car where Carl was waiting with the back passenger door open.

"Good morning, Layla. What a beautiful arrangement. Did you rest well?" He cleared his throat and then smiled showing stained, crooked teeth.

She pretended not to notice and smiled back sincerely at him. "Yes, not too badly thank you. I am eager to go today and am very grateful that you have asked me."

"Of course, you're not only Anna's friend but our friend too. We want to be able to help you." He looked sideways at June and she returned the smile. Almost sinisterly, but Layla was too busy putting her seatbelt on and didn't notice. The drive was pleasant enough and they reached the Hospice in just over an hour. The facility with its rich architectural charm and elegance was located on four acres just outside the city. Layla was glad that it wasn't a sterile hospital setting. They were warmly greeted once inside and shown to Anna's room which was on the main floor with a view of the grounds. She was lying in bed covered with her familiar blankets wearing an oxygen mask as the IV fed her morphine slowly for the pain. June and Carl waited outside to allow them some time together. Layla walked over to her and placed the flowers on the table before taking her hand in hers.

"Anna, it's me, Layla. I miss you so much." She felt her hand move first and then her eyes flickered. Perhaps more of a soft fluttering like the fragile wings of a butterfly, but they didn't open.

"I brought a book that I know you'll love. Let me read it to you." She let go of Anna's frail hand to extract the book from her bag. Opening it to the first page she began to read each inspiring poem in her pleasant voice, moved to tears. After some time, June walked over to the bed.

"Hi Anna. We hope you're comfortable here." Anna seemed to writhe under the blankets after hearing her voice and then began to moan.

"I think that we should call a nurse, she seems like she is in great pain." To see her friend in such discomfort was unbearable. Carl left and brought in the nurse to attend to her.

"I think that we should all go and grab some lunch. We can give her some time to rest and come back afterwards." He licked his lips in anticipation.

June nodded. "Sounds like a good idea Carl." Layla just wanted to stay but the nurse assured her that she would rest while they were gone. She added more water to the flowers, then placed them back on the table before putting her coat on. Carl drove to a steakhouse not too far from the Hospice and they were seated in a comfortable booth within moments of arriving. Layla wasn't hungry as she gazed at the menu but June and Carl seemed famished. The male server, whose name was Logan came shortly to take their drink orders.

"I'll have a large draft beer." Carl piped up first before the ladies, clearing his throat after he spoke.

Layla added. "Just water is fine for me, thank you."

June put down the drink menu and smiled at the young server. "I think a margarita sounds good." It didn't take long before their drinks arrived. Carl and June each ordered steak and lobster with baked potatoes and Ceaser salads. Layla, just a small salad with dressing on the side.

"Can you bring us some bread too please to nibble on, and butter!" Carl took a big drink of beer after toasting June. She sipped her frosty beverage through the straw quickly, smacking her lips.

"It was really nice seeing Anna. I know her situation isn't the best, but just being here shows how much we care about her." June then licked the coarse sugar rim off of the edge of her glass and ordered another one.

"Yes, it means the world to me to be close to her today." Layla was uncomfortable watching them guzzle their drinks, but she still felt gratitude towards them for bringing her.

"Here we are everyone. Hope you enjoy!" Logan, accompanied by another server set down the meals and left them to enjoy their lunch. Both Carl and June demolished the food on their plates without even looking at Layla who took only a few miniscule bites of the salad. They pulled the meat from the lobster like birds of prey stuffing it into their ready mouths after coating it with the melted butter. The sheen on their fingers met the knuckles. When finished, they ordered warm brownie sundaes for dessert and afterwards the server brought the hefty bill.

"Who's the lucky one that gets to pay for the feast today?" His mouth was mocking, but he was hoping for a decent tip. Neither June or Carl said anything as Layla spoke up without hesitation.

"I'll take care of the bill. Afterall, you were kind enough to take me today." She looked in her purse for her wallet and drew it out with a smile.

"Are you sure Layla? We could help you pay if you want." June held her breath, and released it exuberantly when she responded.

"Yes, I insist." She was shocked at the inflated amount of the bill, but remained poised as she estimated the tip. After tapping her credit card for payment, she tucked it carefully back into her wallet and placed it into her tote bag. Both of the vultures watched contentedly.

She was relieved to be back with her dear friend Anna and read more to her as she laid peacefully in her bed. As before, she seemed troubled when she heard June's voice or Carl's. Her eyelids trembled and her body shook with contractions as Layla held her hand. When it was time to go, they said their goodbyes first and went out to speak with the doctor, leaving Layla alone with her.

She leaned in to kiss her forehead tenderly, smoothing back her hair with tears in her eyes.

"Don't trust them!" It was a mere croak, but Layla heard it.

"Pardon me Anna. What did you say?" She put her face close to hers hearing the gentle hum of the oxygen from her mask. But that was all that she said and it troubled Layla, gnawing at her as they drove back to Sarnia. She called Chloe when she arrived home and told her about the visit, leaving out the lavish meal part because she didn't want to make an issue of it. Afterwards, she went to bed early still feeling unsettled and slept fretfully to the early morning.

Chapter 12

Layla awoke to new fallen snow as she opened her bedroom curtains in her cozy, floral patterned house coat. She thought about Anna as she made her way to the bathroom, still wondering what she was trying to tell her. Running the bath water, she placed her hand underneath and adjusted it until it was a pleasant temperature. Carefully, she stepped inside and allowed the warmth of the water to caress her body in both mind and spirit. She relaxed until the water became tepid, then pulled the plug and dried herself off. Once dressed in a casual pair of pants and cozy sweater, she arranged her hair into the typical style and made her way downstairs. The doorbell rang just as she reached the landing and she peered out to see June standing on the porch dressed in an oversized ski jacket and warm boots while her husband Carl cleared the snow from her driveway.

Puzzled, Layla answered the door. "Good morning, June, come in please." She marched in quickly without stomping her boots off and large clumps of snow melted on the mat as the warm air collided with it.

"Thanks. Boy, is it a cold one out there!" Rubbing her hands together, she removed her boots after Layla took her coat from her. She then placed it securely on a hook on the hall tree.

"Is everything alright?" She walked with June to the kitchen to make her a cup of tea and invited her to sit down at the table.

June sighed heavily, almost forcefully. "I am afraid that we have some bad news, Layla. Anna passed away in the night. Her doctor called this morning to let us know." She took a big mouthful of tea after adding a splash of cream and two heaping teaspoons of sugar.

"Oh, no! That's dreadful news. My heart is heavy with grief." Layla began to cry and June stood up to comfort her, tapping her hand repetitively on her back. One eye on the cookie jar.

"If it's any consolation, the doctor said that she died peacefully without any pain. Now, she won't have to suffer anymore. Do you have some of those special home baked cookies of yours?" Her eyes were darting hungrily around the kitchen.

Layla raised her brow slightly at the horrible timing, but put a few from the cookie jar onto a delicately patterned plate for her. She ate them with no regard to tidiness or crumbs as the fragments fell to her lap.

"Does her son know? He'll be devastated." She was twiddling her hands over and over trying to make sense of it all.

Talking with her mouth full, she answered. "Yes, the doctor contacted him first and he is coming back right away to make the arrangements. Carl spoke with him a little while ago. Felix has asked us to stay on and continue caring for the house in the meantime."

"How sad this all is. Will you please inform me of the funeral details when they are arranged? Actually, I would love to speak with

Felix if you would please provide him with my number?"

"Of course. I'll be in touch soon." As she stood up, the loose crumbs fell to the floor from her pants. Layla locked the front door after she left and watched her trudge back over the new fallen snow as she cried softly for the friend that she lost. In the kitchen, she swept up the crumbs all the while fussing and called Chloe telling her about Anna.

"I'm so sorry to hear that Gran. She was a lovely woman and a good friend to you."

"Yes, I'm just heartbroken. I was hoping to see her again, one last time." Layla blew her nose into the white handkerchief that belonged to Winston.

"It's nice that you were able to visit with her yesterday. I am going to cancel my patients for the next several days and come down. I'll stay as long as you need me." Chloe felt terrible for her Gran.

"No, please just come after you finish with your appointments. I certainly don't want you changing everything for me." She was all that she had now.

"I insist Gran. And you know just how stubborn I am. I'll see you as soon as I can."

Gran felt consoled by her granddaughter. "Thank you, Chloe, I love you!"

"And I love you. Bye for now." Chloe arrived three and a half hours later with a suitcase and some takeout food for them to share. They sat in the formal dining room eating the pizza on fancy porcelain plates and enjoying a glass of red wine. Both were talking about unfortunate Anna and her son who was finally coming back now. But it was too late. His precious mother was gone.

"I find it peculiar that Felix hasn't been home in over a year to visit her, especially when she was diagnosed with cancer. And missing Christmas with his mother, that just doesn't seem like him. Anna told me that he was volunteering in Africa a few months before then. I remember him when he was just a young lad, very kind and sweet. He was the apple of his mother's eye and he loved her just as much."

"Maybe he just couldn't get away, but that does sound odd. I understand his passion for work and helping others, but this is his mother." Chloe couldn't comprehend any of it either.

Layla took another sip of the fragrant red wine and reminisced further. "I found an old number for him that he had given me in case of emergency, but it is no longer in service. He must have changed it. Do you remember the Christmas before last when we all sat right here at this table enjoying a dinner that we prepared together? Anna couldn't have been happier with Felix home for the holidays. Who would have known that she would be stricken with cancer so soon afterwards."

"We just never know unfortunately. It was a happy time. After we stuffed ourselves like turkeys, we enjoyed a walk around the neighborhood admiring the festive lights. Then, when we returned, we indulged ourselves again with dessert!" They both laughed together like young school girls.

Gran dabbed at her eyes with her napkin. "How delightful it was to play Scrabble until the wee hours before we all hugged goodnight. I miss her so much. I long for so many of our loved ones now, but I'm thankful that I have you Chloe."

"I am especially grateful for such a wonderful grandmother like you. We make great memories together Gran and will continue to do so." Chloe got up from the table and went to embrace her. She kissed her rosy cheek. They brought their glasses of wine and sat in front of the fireplace on the two cozy chairs. It was formerly wood burning, but Layla wanted convenience so she had it converted to gas several years back. The flames were not only warm, but hypnotic and they both fell silent for a few moments. Each turned in early that evening hoping to hear news of Anna's funeral arrangements soon. Chloe slept in the next day, feeling tranquil in her old bedroom. Rubbing her eyes, she wrapped herself in the fuzzy robe and stuck her feet into slippers before heading downstairs to the kitchen.

"Banana, chocolate chip pancakes! I knew I smelled something delectable. Yum!" She could hardly contain her enthusiasm as Layla placed the plate in front of her. Chloe reached for the maple syrup and streamed ribbons of the sweet mixture over the tall stack. "Thank you, Gran."

Layla beamed and her heart felt like it was full like a balloon, only with love instead of air. It was a sheer joy to please her granddaughter and what she lived for most now. These times reminded her of Arabella and how she loved pancakes dearly. Visions of her dripping the syrup down the front of her made her wistful. "You're welcome, enjoy them." After they finished, Chloe wanted to go ice skating at the outdoor rink with a pretty view of the lake. Layla didn't skate anymore so she bundled up in her long parka with the furry hood to sit and watch with some hot apple cider. Warming her hands on the cup, she watched as Chloe flitted around the rink. Memories of Arabella sprang to her mind once more. What a talented figure skater she was, astounding all who watched her. Chloe inherited so much from her mother including her warm personality and good nature. Her porcelain skin and light brown colored hair was a gift also. As she skated by her Gran, Chloe waved with glee. Wearing pink earmuffs and a navy ski jacket, she was not only graceful, but a vision of loveliness.

They heard from June and Carl a couple of days later and it was not what they were expecting. Both were told that cremation had already taken place. Anna's son Felix had taken her remains back to Sweden with him to disperse there where she was born. They also told Layla and Chloe that it had been her dying wish to her son for this to take place after her death.

"But, why? Her husband Jordan is resting here in Sarnia and that is where she should be. Beside him, her one love!" Layla's eyes were like wildfire, her heart beating out of control like a broken drum.

"I asked Felix to speak with you about her plans. He'll contact you as soon as he is able." June glanced sideways at her tense husband who seemed uncomfortable with multiple beads of perspiration mounting on his brow. He cleared his throat. With a raspy voice like a hand saw cutting through wood, he spoke. "Yes, just be patient and wait for his call." But they heard nothing from Felix and after a week, Layla encouraged Chloe to think about her practice and going back to her patients. No matter how much she loved having her around, she knew that she mustn't be selfish. Her granddaughter had a flourishing career and she wasn't going to ruin it.

"But Gran, I don't want to leave you now." Chloe pouted.

"I'll be fine, don't worry your pretty little head about little old me. And I'm sure that everything will all make sense soon." Layla held onto the doorframe fearing that she would crumble to the floor like one of the snickerdoodle cookies as she waved goodbye to Chloe. She watched her as she backed down the driveway waving and then unwillingly closed the door when she was out of sight. As Chloe drove home, she was grateful for June and her husband Carl. They helped her Gran with the snow removal in the winter and grass cutting in the summer. At first, they declined renumeration when she offered, but since worked out a payment method via e-transfers. And, they both promised her that they would check in on her Gran daily which was reassuring. She felt torn between the work that she loved and her Gran, wishing she would move to Oakville with her.

Layla finished taking the last batch of cookies from the oven and left them to cool on the metal racks on the countertop. Grandma Annette's snickerdoodles sure were popular, especially with June and Carl. He had just finished clearing the snow from her driveway and she wanted to thank them with their desired treat. After they were cool, she placed them in a pretty tin and tied a matching ribbon around it. Donning her winter boots and coat, she wrapped a velvety cashmere scarf around her neck. Then, she made her way next door with the sweet confection and knocked firmly on the front door. June opened it within minutes and welcomed her inside as Layla stamped the snow off of her boots. She took her coat from her and hung it inside of the hall closet, the one where Anna always placed hers. Layla saw that her coats were still inside along with some footwear on the floor. She swallowed with effort, the lump that had risen in her throat.

"I made some freshly baked cookies for you and Carl to enjoy. Thank you so much for helping with the grounds, I wouldn't be able to shovel anymore. Winston, my husband used to take care of all that along with the lawn. I loved tending to the gardens; I found it very therapeutic."

June took the tin hungrily from her, almost clawing it from her hands. "Thanks a bunch, Layla, these are so good. I could eat them by the dozens! Come, sit down for a moment and we'll talk. There is a small box of keepsakes from Anna for you as well." The living room was almost exactly as Anna had decorated it, except for most of the knick knacks which had disappeared.

Layla was perched on the edge of the sofa. "Have you any news or heard from Felix?"

"No, last time we spoke, he told us that he had a backlog of patients to see. He seemed depressed about not being with his mother when she passed. Carl thought that we should just give him some more time." June gingerly untied the satin ribbon, lifted the lid and took out a cookie as Carl entered the room.

"Hello Layla. How are you?" He was always clearing his throat like there was something caught in it.

"Fine, Carl and yourself?" She watched as he looked uneasy and cleared his throat again repeatedly.

"Good." His head was hung low and his eyes kept darting back and forth from Layla to his wife.

"Thank you for taking care of the snow. There certainly seemed like a ton for you to remove. Good thing that you have the snowblower." She smiled gratefully at him.

"Yes, it comes in very handy. I have some more to do outside." He coughed and then excused himself without taking a cookie.

Layla watched as June ate another snickerdoodle and then brushed the crumbs to the floor with her hands.

"Well, I think that I will go now. If you hear from Felix, please let me know." As she got up from the chair that Anna always sat on, she noticed the small pillow that she embroidered and picked it up. *"Home Sweet Home!"* Her fingers stroked the raised stitches that had been painstakingly done so many years ago. Sighing, she placed it back gently on the chair and made her way to the front hallway. Just then, the phone rang and June excused herself to answer it. Layla could see Carl shovelling the sidewalk as she sat on the seat to put her boots on. She could hear June's voice in the distance so she opened the closet to fetch her coat. Pulling it from the hanger, she noticed that her scarf had fallen to the floor inside. Bending down to pick it up, she saw what looked like two cardboard boxes in the corner and an envelope with Anna's name on it. Her hand was shaking as she reached for it and her heartbeat felt as though it was pounding in her head and not her chest. She gasped and covered her mouth with her unstable hand as she read the first few lines of the letter inside.

Dear Ms. Anna Wagner

It is with the deepest regret that we must inform you that your son Felix died of malaria while volunteering in Africa. As per his wishes, we have processed the cremation and are sending his ashes back to you for proper burial.

The date on the top confirmed that it was written the January before last. No wonder he didn't visit, he wasn't alive. Horrified, she steadied herself by holding onto the handle of the closet door. Feeling like she could pass out, Layla closed her eyes and took long, deep breaths releasing the air slowly threw her lips. It sounded to her like a strong, gusty wind in inclement weather. June's unrestrained voice talking on the phone brought her back to the present and she quickly stuffed the letter into her coat pocket and put it on. Curious, she bent down and pulled one of the small cardboard boxes to look closer at it. She was reeling when she realized that it was the cremated remains of Anna's son Felix. *But what did the other box contain?* Peering at the label, she almost fainted when she saw Anna's name on it. Pushing both of the boxes back into the corner of the closet, Layla stumbled out the door with her scarf in hand, hurrying to her home.

Inside, she locked the door behind her and leaned against it trying to catch her breath. Tears filled her eyes blurring her vision, she was shaking and felt clammy. She placed her coat on an available hook on the carved hall tree and hurried up the stairs, stumbling with the letter in her hand. She could feel the pain radiating in her left knee, but forced herself up, holding onto the banister. She sat on the bed feeling winded and opened the letter up again to finish reading it. Covering her mouth in shock, she stuffed it back into the envelope and placed it in the chest at the end of the bed. Her hand caressed the soft blue blanket that belonged to sweet Lincoln as she covered the letter with it. Rushing back downstairs, she ran to the kitchen to call her granddaughter. Before she could reach Chloe, June was at her door knocking with vigor.

Taking a deep breath, Layla wiped her tears and smoothed down her hair before opening the door with a pretentious smile. "June, what are you doing here?" She kept her hands hidden so she wouldn't see them trembling.

"You left before I could give you the items that Anna wanted you to have." She held the box out for her to see and then made her way inside.

"Oh, yes, I just thought that I would leave you to your phone call. Thank you for bringing them to me. I will forever cherish everything from her." Holding her breath, she waited for her to leave but she insisted on carrying the box in for her. "Just place it on the dining room table and I'll look through it and reminisce later." Layla was sure that she was going to faint.

"Okay, sure. There you go then." As she lifted her hands from the box, Layla caught sight of something sparkling. On her right hand was the heirloom ring that Anna had been saving to give Felix when he proposed. Passed down for many generations, the ring was priceless with its multiple carats of diamonds. In the centre was a majestic five carat diamond surrounded by natural round and pear-shaped diamonds. Her eyes never left June's hand, hypnotized by Anna's ring.

Gasping, her hand flew to her mouth in protection of her dear friend's legacy.

"That ring! Why are you wearing it?" She could barely speak clearly and her voice sounded like someone else's, not hers. Deep and urgently desperate.

June looked taken aback for a moment, then composed herself. "It's stunning, isn't it? Anna insisted that I have it. I tried to refuse, but she wanted to give it to me. She said as a present for taking such good care of her." Her stout fingers stroked the piece delicately as Layla watched, extremely disturbed. She was fuming. The heirloom piece was invaluable. Anna had only worn it on special occasions; she cherished it very much. She had told her the history behind it and how dear it was. Anna was looking forward to the day when her son would find true love and then place it on her finger. How devastating that neither would live to see the day.

Layla recalled how her eyes would light up at the thought of grandchildren. Now, the remains of both mother and son were hidden in boxes in the closet, without a funeral. Cast away like a pair of old, worn-out shoes. Suddenly, she began slurring her words and felt numbness on her entire right side of her face and body. June was speaking to her, but she couldn't understand a word. She was also seeing double and feeling dizzy. Layla fell against the wall as June watched, her fingers still finessing the stolen ring that she wore in a mocking way.

"What's wrong Layla? Come and sit down." She walked her carefully to the sofa noticing that the right side of her face was drooping. She instantly knew that she was having a stroke but waited hours before calling the ambulance. Watching her lay there like a deer begging the coyote not to eat her entertained her. Her eyes were venomous as she realized the mistake of wearing the ring and allowing her to see it. Normally, she would take it off when visiting with Layla, but she forgot this time. She loved wearing it and admiring it. It made her feel like a millionaire. Or perhaps a queen. She deserved it after caring for the old lady.

Finally, when June got around to calling 911, she had wasted very valuable time. Every moment was crucial with a stroke victim and she knew it. The ambulance arrived and took Layla to the hospital where she was given emergency IV medicine along with a CT scan.

June called Chloe when she got to the hospital and explained the situation to her. Conjuring up the crocodile tears came easy to her, both she and Carl stayed in the waiting room until Chloe arrived.

She was dishevelled and the worry that she wore on her face told of the powerful love she had for her Gran.

"Where is she? Can I see her?" Chloe was out of breath.

June hugged her and wiped her fake tears, then blew her nose. "No, not yet. The doctors will speak to us when they know more. Right now, they're treating her. Have a seat for now."

Chloe was stunned. "What happened? Gran is in good health. I just spoke with her and she was well."

"I don't know. I brought over a box of special keepsakes that Anna left to her and found her slurring her words. As soon as she answered the door, I knew that her symptoms indicated a stroke. So right away I called for an ambulance." Carl cleared his throat nervously and squirmed like a small child in his chair as she embellished the story.

"Thank goodness you were there, otherwise she may have not received the care as quickly." Chloe gave her a big hug, grateful again for the help that they gave to her Gran. But if only she knew the menacing truth.

"Yes, with my nursing background, I saw just how delicate her situation was. Time is of the essence." She smiled a dishonest smile that looked malevolent and dried her eyes as Carl cleared his throat again. He left and returned with hot coffee for them as they waited impatiently.

Hours later, the team of doctors came out to update them on Layla's condition. The head of the surgical team, Dr. Nelson introduced himself and shook her hand.

"How is my Gran?" Chloe tried to remain strong, but she felt as though even a small draft could cause her to fall over. Perhaps, just a mere whisper of breath. She braced herself for the news.

"Her condition is extremely serious. She has had an Ischemic stroke which occurs when a blood vessel supplying blood to the brain is obstructed. We have successfully removed the clot and she is now resting. The extent of the damage is questionable right now and we will have a better idea as she recovers."

"May I see her doctor?" Chloe was confused by her Gran's diagnosis. She always ate healthy and kept active on a daily basis.

"Of course, I'll show you to her room." He left her then to visit as June and Carl stood in the hall and eavesdropped outside the door.

"Gran, it's Chloe. Don't worry about anything, I'll be here for you. You're going to be okay. I love you so much Gran." She laid her head on the bed and cried as she held her hand. The stroke damage was obvious on her face with her eyelid and corner of her mouth drooping. Chloe asked them to set up a cot and stayed the night with her, sleeping fretfully. The nursing staff was attentive and checked on her frequently throughout the evening.

On the fourth day, Layla began rehabilitation including physical, speech and occupational therapy. She was having difficulty with memory skills as well as her speaking. Walking proved challenging also, so she used a wheelchair which was heartbreaking to see. The damage inflicted by the stroke was higher than they originally predicted and regrettably, it would be a long recovery for Layla.

Chapter 13

June and Carl were a godsend offering to move in and care for Layla so she could recover in her own home. Chloe took a leave of absence from her optometry office to be there for her Gran. Doc Benson as always, was extremely sympathetic and understanding to her needs. June came up with the brilliant idea to convert the dining room into a main floor bedroom for her so she would be able to use her wheelchair on the whole main floor. There was also a full bathroom adjacent to the dining room for her to use as well. Layla could not form her words to speak coherently and was unable to take anymore than a few steps even with help. Chloe was optimistic that with continued treatment, her Gran would fully recover back to her usual self.

Two months later, Layla was recovering but gradually. She could now take a few steps using her cane with her left hand, but her right side was not making as much progress. Her face still projected the droopiness related with a stroke. And the articulation with words was still far from comprehensible. June cooked and cleaned for them offering help where needed and Carl continued caring for the exterior of the property. Both helped with appointments which eased the load immensely.

June carefully approached Chloe one day as Layla was resting. She set down her coffee cup on the small round table to listen to what she had to say.

"I wanted for you to know that if you would like to go back to your practice, Carl and I will hold the fort down here. I understand how much you love your Gran, but your career is important also. You can be assured that her care will be top priority and we will continue to take her to all of the physiotherapy and doctor's appointments. You could come back on weekends to visit."

June tried to look sincere as she waited for Chloe to respond.

"I don't know about leaving her. Work was my whole world before my Gran's stroke, but now everything has changed. She needs me, and I don't want for her to think that I am abandoning her when she needs help the most." Tears sprang to her eyes as she reached for her cup and took a small sip of her coffee. What June was telling her seemed unfathomable.

June argued the point more. "You have to ask yourself what she would want for you to do if she could tell you. Do you think that she wants you to give up your career and everything that you have worked hard for now?"

"I know her response. My bags would be packed today if she knew how long I have been off work. That doesn't matter though, because she is incapable of making those choices unfortunately. And I would never forgive myself if anything else happens to her."

"Just keep it in your mind, okay? That it is an option for you." June just wanted her to go back to her home in Oakville and to get out of her hair. She took both coffee cups to the sink, rinsed them and placed them in the dishwasher. Chloe stood up to check on her Gran.

By the end of the week, Layla seemed to be able to nod her head slightly when asked questions which offered more hope of her recovering. There was a look of fear prominently in her eyes. The physiotherapy was going well and she had the best team helping with her recovery. Chloe was meeting with some of her patients via virtual visits which only made her feel more conflicted. She missed what she did but also wanted to support her Gran. Doc Benson and she spoke on a daily basis with him keeping her up to date on her patients. Glenda, their receptionist, called her weekly to chat and she hung up still thinking about what June suggested days ago. After a night filled with tossing and turning, she decided to return to work four days a week and spend the other three with her Gran. She spoke with June about her decision that morning and she seemed ecstatic, almost relieved.

"That sounds like a perfect idea Chloe! Carl and I will assist with all of Layla's appointments and physiotherapy. Don't you worry about anything!" Her face looked like a decade of worry had been wiped off of it as she displayed a smile flaunting discolored teeth. She would have jumped for joy at that point, but it would have taken so much effort.

"I can never thank you enough. I would move Gran back home with me, but I know that it isn't her desire to leave here. Her happiness is very important to me; she must have the best." Her eyes were moist and June reluctantly stood up to get her the box of tissues from the table. No rest for the wicked.

When Chloe left on Sunday evening, her heart felt like a chunk of lead. She cried the whole way home thinking about her Gran. She was all that she had, everything to her. Life was cruel, but she had to forage on. Each song that came on the radio reminded her of her family and instead of taking her mind off of her pain, she became further grief-stricken. The drive went fairly smoothly, apart from some heavier traffic on the 401. Inhaling deeply, she blew out the breath through her mouth when she reached her home. The compressed air sounding like a beach ball deflating. She parked her car in the driveway and removed her overnight bag from the trunk. After pressing the fob and hearing the high-pitched beep, she walked wearily to her front door observing the double car garage. Chloe had never parked inside of it, even in the most brutal of winters. She chose to clean the piles of snow off instead and sit in her frigid car while it warmed up. She loathed the garage actually. It reminded her of the devastating tragedy that took place so many years ago, robbing her of her entire family. Regardless of her car being electric, she couldn't bring herself to drive inside.

After making a light snack, she went outside to water the flowers in her urns. Glenda had cared for them while she was gone and did a fine job. The blooms of purple, yellow and white cascaded down the sides of the black cast iron. Chloe was enthralled by the loveliness as she gave each one a healthy drink of cool water. Fortunately, the previous owners had installed a watering system for the lawn so it always looked immaculate.

That night, she was haunted by visions of her Gran struggling to speak, then of June and Carl. She couldn't quite place her finger on it, but something was amiss. Morning came before she was ready for it and she dragged herself out of bed complaining. After checking with June, she stepped into the shower and then dressed quickly. Popping some toast down in the toaster, Chloe poured herself a cup of coffee with cream. Cupping both of her hands around the mug, she was deep in thought until the toast popped up, causing her to jump. She buttered it and cut it in half, then opened her laptop to review her schedule. After a few bites, she pushed the plate away. She loved her work and treating the patients. Chloe was fortunate to have caught the early symptoms of a detached retina in one of her patients They were referred to an ophthalmologist immediately, thus saving the patients sight in that eye. Chloe chose to walk to work and Glenda greeted her kindly when she arrived at the optometry office.

"Good morning, Chloe. It's always a joy to see you back. How is your Gran, any progress?"

She shook her head. "Sadly, no. I pray for the day when she'll be back to her usual self again."

"Well, don't lose hope. She just needs more time." Glenda gave her a hug which she truly needed, she felt like a second mother to her. Chloe opened her office door and a sense of tranquility took over. It was strange, but she felt close to her mother when she was there now. After putting her purse in the desk drawer, she walked over to the bookcase. She gazed at the carved wooden box for a few seconds before picking it up cautiously with both hands. Her fingers caressed the engravings as memories of Oliver pierced her thoughts. Before she could change her mind, she opened the lid and peered inside for the first time in weeks. She didn't actually expect to see the three sand dollars inside, did she? No, her heart felt splintered recalling how each was placed on top of the caskets. Her mother's, father's and Ariana's. The sand dollars were gone, buried like her beloved family. But she still had her Gran and that was why she wanted to help her to get better. There was a soft knock on her door and she hurriedly set the precious box back in its place on the shelf.

"Chloe, Philip Kennedy is here."

"Thank you, Glenda, I'll be right out." She dried her eyes and proceeded on with her morning. It was a busy day with just a small lunch break, but she didn't mind. She ate her lunch with Doc Benson and he looked tenderly at her.

"How are you managing Chloe?"

She smiled at him. "Great, I love it here!"

He shook his head slowly. "No, I meant emotionally. Are you struggling with anything that I can help you with? You know that I will try to help you in any way that I can."

Her eyes teared up. "I know that Doc and I couldn't love you more. I am managing. Just when I think that I am okay, the tears start flowing again. It's a never-ending battle."

"You're incredibly courageous. I couldn't be pleased with you." They hugged then and he left her to go back to his office.

Luckily, the days that she worked passed by quickly and before she knew it, she was driving back to Sarnia to be with her Gran on Friday morning. Chloe patted herself on the back and smiled with relief. She did it! She got through the week with her patients and now she could devote all of her time to her Gran. It was early summer; the sun was golden in the sky and the temperature warm like a blanket wrapped around one's body.

The assortment of flower gardens greeted her like giant bouquets as she drove up the concrete driveway and parked. Carl seemed to have a green thumb with the perennials which pleased her. He tended to the vegetable gardens in the back as well as maintaining all of Anna's property. Gran loved her home and Chloe couldn't wait for the day that she could garden again. June greeted her happily as she ran up the steps to the porch and hugged her. Carl went to the car and carried Chloe's luggage upstairs, after clearing his throat, multiple times when speaking to them. June was dressed in a pair of baggy pants and an oversized t shirt that looked as though moths had dined on it. Her eyes were squinty as she forced a smile.

"It's so nice to have you here again. Your Gran is relaxing on the back patio and I know that she is excited to see you!"

"Thank you, June. How has she been?"

"Just a charm. She seems to have adjusted well to the new schedule and her progression with her therapists has been amazing." She bit her lip knowing that it was all a lie. She had cancelled Layla's physiotherapy and other appointments that past week due to a cold. Well, that's what she had told them while pretending to be Chloe.

Chloe felt delighted. "That's wonderful! I can't wait to see her."

There was lemonade and some small nibbles to enjoy on the patio table. Chloe skipped to her Gran who was sitting in her wheelchair and hugged her feeling blissful. She also planted a big kiss on her cheek.

"Oh, Gran, I am so happy to be back here with you! I missed you so much. I'm glad that you're getting better and cannot wait until we can take walks again together. And have our chips under the bridge." Her eyes flinched and she seemed weary as Chloe spoke to her. She bent down and held her hand, waiting for Layla to acknowledge her. What she didn't suspect was that June was giving her muscle relaxers and depressants to delay the healing process. She couldn't have Layla recovering now after everything that she knew. Her face when she saw her wearing Anna's ring displayed not only loyalty to her friend, but contempt towards June. She had never feared anyone really, but sensed a strange power radiate from Layla that she had never felt before. What would she have done if she hadn't had the stroke? It worked out very well for her and Carl. The monthly paycheck was enormous and June wouldn't have anything or anyone ruining it for her. Not even Layla's loving granddaughter.

Chloe looked at June puzzled. "Is she okay? Why isn't she interacting with me?"

"She had a bit of a rough night; I went in to sit with her a few times. She is most likely just tired now. I'm sure that she'll be good as new after her nap." June looked at her from the corner of her eyes, hoping that she wouldn't press her more.

Alarmed, Chloe stood up. "Has she had her lunch?"

"Yes, just before you arrived." She lied, but that's what she did so well now. Chloe helped her to get her Gran comfortably into bed before returning to the sunny patio to sit. She noticed the snickerdoodle cookies and after taking a plate, she placed one on it with some fresh fruit. June poured her some lemonade from a big picture into a large glass and topped it with a slice of lemon.

"Thank you. Did you make the lemonade from scratch?"

"Yes, do you like it?" June was so good at being deceitful, that she even surprised herself.

"Delicious. And the cookies are good as well. The snickerdoodle recipe was my great grandma Annette's and passed down for many generations." Chloe wasn't being insincere; they were decent but something was missing. An ingredient perhaps? She took another bite and let the cookie dissolved slowly on her tongue before it hit her. *Love!* That was the missing ingredient and without it, they were well, just cookies. She helped June tidy up the refreshments and carried the lemonade back to the kitchen, placing it into the refrigerator. When she opened the stainless-steel garbage pail with her foot to dispose of the waste, she saw two empty cartons of lemonade inside. June lied about making the lemonade she thought wryly. She removed her foot quickly, allowing the shiny lid to close securing the secret inside. She went down the hallway and looked in on her Gran who was still resting.

"Gran seems to be sleeping longer than usual. Should we wake her now?"

"Give her some more time. She must be especially tired today. She worked very hard this week on her physiotherapy." June looked at Carl who cleared his throat while Chloe watched. He seemed to be fidgety all of the time. And all that throat clearing!

A Gran Scheme

Finally, Layla woke up and Chloe was there waiting to be with her Gran. She was reading quietly curled up in a chair by the window while she rested.

She got up and went to the bed. "Well, hi there sleepyhead! How do you feel?"

Chloe watched her closely for any signs of communication. All she saw was blinking and a twitch of her left hand which she took and caressed. After giving her Gran a drink of water thorough the paper straw that she poured fresh for her, she offered to read. She brought one of the murder mystery books that she had purchased from the bookstore over and sat down on the bed. She began reading the captivating story, finishing after three Chapters when June called them for dinner. She came in with Carl to help Layla with the washroom duties and then they gathered at the kitchen table. The apricot glazed chicken with roasted potatoes and vegetables looked appealing. What June lacked in baking; she made up for in cooking. It was scrumptious! Chloe helped to feed her Gran who she thought was truly retracting in progress. She couldn't figure it out, but something seemed off to her. Each time she drove back home to Oakville, it stole a piece of her heart.

When Layla's telephone rang early Monday morning, June was quick to pick it up, setting it to speaker phone.

"Dawson residence."

"Hello, this is Dr. Nelson. I am hoping to speak with Ms. Chloe Burke please." His voice was professional, but seemingly urgent.

Swallowing a lump the size of a pebble in her throat she began to speak. "This is she; how can I help you Dr. Nelson?"

"I am quite alarmed that Ms. Layla Dawson has not been attending her physical or occupational therapy for months. Her team of therapists only wish to see her recover and have expressed concern."

"Oh, how kind of you all! I did call several weeks ago to inform everyone that she is continuing her care in Oakville with me. After a brief illness, we both thought that she would better flourish with me. I'm sorry, I thought that you knew." She looked up from the outrageous lie to see Layla watching her from the doorway of her room. There was no question about her comprehension, her eyes showed immense horror and contempt towards June. She marched over to her, pushed the chair inside and closed the door briskly before returning to the call.

"No, I wasn't aware of the changes and wish that we could have discussed this more. It is important that her new therapists as well as doctor continue the schedule that we have been working with." He sighed heavily.

"Again, my Gran is receiving the very best care possible. Thank you for calling Dr. Nelson. She placed the phone back on the cradle and scoffed at the old-fashioned land line. Most of the time Layla used the tablet for calls, but insisted on keeping the other telephone to which she had since Winston and she purchased the home.

By the end of July, her Gran was still not making great advancement and Chloe made a note to contact her doctors as well as therapists. She wanted answers as to why she wasn't developing more. She brought her a writing tablet to use for communication and showed her how to use it. There was a stylus to write with and a button to press to clear it afterwards. Each day Chloe made sure to put it on her lap as she sat in her wheelchair, praying that she would write something.

After breakfast, she went up to shower leaving Layla in the living room to gaze out the window. Carl was mowing the lawn, cutting it horizontally to make a checkerboard pattern. He had just finished Anna's property earlier. Layla could hear the whirling sound of the motor through the window and thought of Winston. Lifting her left hand, she took the fine pen and began writing the letters to make words. June came in to see her when she finished the clearing the breakfast dishes, looking dishevelled.

Layla's quick movement caught her attention and suspicious, she grabbed the writing tablet from her lap.

"Well, what do we have here?" Her face glowered as she looked at it. Anger filled her veins instead of blood. It looked like fine chicken scratch, but it was legible. *"JUNE EVIL"*. She quickly pressed the button to erase it when she heard Chloe making her way down the staircase. Quickly, she wrote *"LOVE YOU"* as messy as she could and shoved it back onto Layla's lap. Stepping away, she busied herself, straightening the cushions of the sofa so not to look distraught, which she was.

Chloe made her way over to her Gran and sat across from her on one of the wing chairs. Noticing the writing on the board, she took it from her.

"Oh, my goodness! That's wonderful and I love you Gran. Let's try some more."

June intervened immediately. "Sorry, Chloe but she must go to the washroom first." Her large arms, bulky like a mans, wheeled the chair into Layla's room and shut the door. She raised her hand, wanting to slap her but stopped. The old bird somehow avoided taking her pills and she was going to get to the bottom of it. She found the last night's medication under her pillow and the morning dose wrapped in tissue in her wheelchair. She heard Carl come in from his yard work and beckoned him into Layla's room.

"Where is Chloe?" June whispered, she didn't want her listening.

Carl answered after clearing his throat. "She went out back to tend to the gardens for a bit."

"Good, we got a problem here. Granny hasn't been taking her pills." Casting a mean look towards Layla, she felt like choking the old woman. "Watch her for me, I'll be right back." June slithered down the hallway to the kitchen like a venomous snake where she caught sight of Chloe crouched down working outside. Quickly, she brought the small mortar and pestle back with her. Prudently, she grinded the pills that were discarded in the tissue and then mixed the powder with a touch of warm tap water. Taking an oral syringe from the package in the bathroom, she slowly drew the mixture up into the base.

"Give me a hand now Carl." He looked uncomfortable and cleared his throat.

"What are we going to do? I don't think that she's going to like that." He looked frightened and beads of sweat were running from his forehead into the corner of his eyes causing him to blink. Not from just mowing the lawns in the heat, but from sheer terror.

"Just shut up and do as I say. Hold her head back and pinch her nose while I squeeze the medication into her throat." Aside from the throttling sound of Carl's throat clearing frequently, the room was eerily silent. June cupped her hand around Layla's mouth as she injected the concoction and watched as her eyes became huge with fright. There was an almost inaudible gurgling sound and then it was over. After just a short period, Layla was back in her comatose-like state and June was deeply satisfied. Before she brought her out, she took the writing tablet and stuffed it under the mattress. She really felt like driving it over with her car, crushing it to pieces. They joined Chloe in the backyard and watched her garden until lunch time. Carl helped to pull weeds as June lazed with an icy cold drink. She wished that it had some booze in it but she had to keep her mind clear, especially after the morning she had.

The next evening, everyone enjoyed an astounding display of fireworks from the front porch while eating popcorn and drinking ginger ale which was Layla's favorite. The bright collection of sparkling lights delighted the eyes reminding Chloe of her families Canada Day parties in the backyard. The illuminations held extra appeal as they reflected off of the water tricking the mind. All of a sudden, she had to excuse herself and went inside to the washroom to cry. An explosion of tears, comparable to the colorful fireworks released from being pent up for so long. Chloe was exhausted. After flushing her face with cool water and straightening her hair, she went back outside to sit close to her Gran. Her brief but unexpected departure did not go unnoticed from June's intense scrutiny.

"Are you alright sweetie?" June put on her best sympathetic face encouraging her to share her innermost feelings.

"Yes, just some old family memories came flooding back. Each Canada Day, my parents would hold a backyard celebration with all of the neighbors. There were tables of food, dad would barbeque and afterwards, we would gather our front for the fireworks." She looked at her Gran and noticed that her eyes were also damp. She took the tissue that she had tucked into her sleeve and gently blotted her eyes. Was she thinking about all of the special times too, she wondered?

After Gran was in bed sleeping, Chloe typed several questions that she was proposing to ask her doctors. Perhaps they could shed some light into why she wasn't speaking, walking and eating by herself after several months. The next weekend was her Gran's birthday and she wanted to plan an exciting time for her. She knew how healing pets were and she had adopted a young therapy dog to be a companion for her. The

Yorkshire Terrier whose name was Iris was almost one year old and just under 7 pounds. Her Gran's favorite perennial was the gorgeous iris and she felt it a godsend that this puppy came into their lives. She loved the deep purple hue with the yellow accent and treasured that the three upright petals stood for faith, wisdom and valor. The size was perfect for a lap dog and she knew that her Gran would love that. She was so busy with the adoption and planning her party that she forgot to call Dr. Nelson's office to speak about her concerns.

She picked up the little yorkie on Friday before she left armed with all of the necessities that a new pet owner would require. There was a small crate, food, bowls as well as a harness and leash. She could hardly contain herself as she drove down the highway to Sarnia. This time as she drove up the laneway, her Gran was sitting in her wheelchair waiting for her on the front porch. Carl had built a ramp for the chair to go down. Chloe squealed with glee and then made herself calm down so not to spoil the surprise.

"Hi Gran, happy birthday!" Chloe called out joyfully and waved to her. Afterwards, she opened the rear passenger door to retrieve the surprise. Then, bouncing up the stairs, she set down the crate and hugged her. Breathing deeply the harmony into her lungs that she felt whenever she was with her.

"What in God's name is in there?" June pointed at it and looked highly insulted.

Reaching inside, she gingerly lifted Iris out to meet her new owner.

"Iris, meet Layla, my Gran." Chloe put the sweet little dog on her lap and placed her hand on top to caress her. Layla was bursting with joy, but June was seething. How dare she bring more work for her, cleaning up after a dog was not what she was getting paid for. Well, she'd have to demand more money, wouldn't she?

"Isn't she adorable? I think that a companion is just what my Gran needs right now. And what better than a dog." Giggling, her heart was exploding with delight.

"Just peachy, but who is going to clean up after it?" June despised animals and couldn't relate to why so many people loved them.

"Don't worry, Iris is fully housetrained and hardly ever barks. She won't be a burden at all." Chloe and her Gran already loved her.

Carl cleared his voice excessively sounding like an old Chevy revving up. He looked happily at Chloe. "I'll go to the car and bring your things up to your room." He could already tell that June was stewing about the miniature dog. He actually thought she was cute.

On Saturday, Chloe was planning to take her Gran for an afternoon under the bridge in celebration of her special day. June was forceful in wanting to join them, but Chloe told her that it was their together time. She brushed her Gran's hair and then put in the tortoise shell combs that she liked to wear on each side. After a small swipe of blush and a little lip gloss, Chloe then put the birthday crown on her head. Layla smiled crookedly when she showed her in the mirror and Iris wagged her tail in delight.

"Do you think she looks pretty? Yes, she does!" Chloe scooped up the little dog and hugged it before placing it on her Gran's lap.

The day was absolutely gorgeous and the three of them set off down the street to embark on their birthday celebration for Layla. June scowled at the door watching them as they went, hoping that Chloe would change her mind. But she didn't. It almost seemed that June was her Gran's Siamese twin, but today was the exception.

"Look Gran, there's a big ship coming by!" They stopped out front of the restaurant to watch the massive structure continue under the bridges. The brightly painted red ship was over a 1000 ft long. It was bustling everywhere like a giant celebration and there was a large lineup for the tasty fries. "We'll get ice cream afterwards and sit on our usual bench by the water, okay?" Gran tapped her left hand gently and smiled. Chloe ordered a plate of fish and chips for both of them as well as a ginger ale to go with it. Calvin, Chanel's brother flashed them a smile and waved, then waited on the next customers.

"Well, hello you two! It's wonderful to have you today. Or should I say three! Who's this little friend?" The restaurant was family owned for many decades and now the grandchildren ran it with their children successfully. Chanel smiled a gentle smile knowing of the turbulent past both of them shared. Her parents had always loved Layla, who was kind and generous with them. As did her grandparents who were no longer with them unfortunately. She had sent them a lovely arrangement when they passed away and attended the funeral. Her heart ached for them now with the set back of Layla's stroke.

"Thank you! This is Iris." Chloe pushed back a tendril of hair from her face and tucked it behind her ear. She was wearing a sundress the color of the sky and matching drop earrings.

Chanel was tall and remarkably pretty with long dark blonde hair that she had brushed into a high ponytail for work. Over her shorts and top, she wore a pink apron. "Hi Iris, you're just the cutest! Is someone celebrating a birthday?" She knew by the crown that it was Layla, but enjoyed being playful with her.

"It's my Gran's birthday so we're celebrating with her favorite meal of fish and chips. And afterwards, ice cream, of course!" Chloe beamed as she told her.

"That sounds like the best birthday ever. And it's all on the house, our treat today!"

"Really! What a nice surprise, thank you!"

When their food was ready, Chanel carried everything outside to the table and set it up for them to eat. She even brought straws and napkins.

"Enjoy, see you soon for the ice cream. We have over thirty flavors to choose from today!" Chloe thanked her again and helped her Gran with her food. Both felt the warmth of the sunshine on their backs as the seagulls squawked in their high-pitched voices yearning for a tasty fry. Iris sat on Layla's lap contentedly only requesting water and a small dog treat that they brought with them. Chloe walked her to the grassy area afterwards to do her business and then they went back inside for the frosty treat.

Layla wished desperately that she could speak to her granddaughter, but she could barely nod her head. She had to find a way to tell Chloe of the appalling things that June and Carl were up to. It felt as though she was incoherent most of the time. And she knew now that the medication they were giving her was hindering any recovery. But June was wise to her tricks of removing it from her mouth when she left the room. She was livid when she found out. Chloe wheeled her chair slowly in front of the ice cream counter to help her choose. Tears stung her eyes and it felt like the wind had been knocked out of her when she saw the chocolate or choclate ice cream, Arabella's favorite. It caressed her heart when she watched her eat it, leaving more on her face and clothing than in her tummy. Some memories would never fade. She nodded towards the butterscotch and Chanel made her a huge sundae with butterscotch topping and whipped cream. There was even a cherry on top. Chloe chose rocky road in a cup and they went down to the water to sit. The view was captivating with the eye drawn to the shimmering waves as the boats travelled through. The other side of the border was also busy with people out enjoying the summertime weather and frolicking. Chloe laughed as she picked up the cherry and put it in her Gran's mouth.

June practically pounced on them when they arrived home. She was waiting on the porch like a cheetah ready to leap on its prey as Chloe pushed her up the wooden ramp leading to the porch.

Her lips were pursed. "It's about time, I'd say! You know that Layla tires very easily and requires her medication at proper intervals! You could have put her health at risk."

"It's all fine, June. We had a wonderful afternoon together. And the weather couldn't have been nicer." It was true, a lovely day they shared and the temperature was perfect.

June scoffed inside, but forced a pretentious smile. "I'm glad to hear that. Come Layla, let's get you cleaned up." She reached for the little dog and set it down on the porch with disgust. Chloe picked her up and coddled her on her lap as she sat beside Carl on the diamond lattice settee. He reached over to pet Iris as she licked his hand lovingly.

"I'm glad that you had a special day with your Gran, she deserves it." He cleared his throat nervously.

"Thank you, Carl. It meant so much to both of us and even Iris had fun! Chanel and her family didn't charge us for a thing; she's such a sweetheart." He nodded at her and cleared his throat, then looked down at his hands.

"There is a present for your Gran in her bedroom. I wanted Iris to be able to get up and down from her bed so I purchased dog stairs from the pet store." His hands were toying nervously with each other and Chloe reached out to put her hand on his.

"That is so thoughtful, she'll be touched. Thank you!"

Chapter 14

Perhaps it was the sheer delight that Layla took in the new dog that irritated June the most. But she hated it more everyday. She could absentmindedly leave the back gate open and the little varmint might run away. A slow smile took over her face as she pictured Chloe frantically searching for her as her Gran sat staidly in her wheelchair. Carl helped with Iris while Chloe was away working by taking her outside and for little walks. He wanted Layla to join them as well for fresh air and sunshine, but June wouldn't allow it. So, she stayed inside most of the time parked in front of the living room window or in her bedroom until Chloe came back. Carl didn't recognize his wife anymore. She had metamorphosed into a monster slowly in front of his eyes and he felt helpless.

Meanwhile, in Oakville Chloe balanced her busy schedule at the office in between visits with her Gran. They had countless new patients that heard just how compassionate the optometry office was and were fully booked on a daily basis. Chloe had a half an hour for lunch to relax and sat with Glenda in front of the French balcony. The small bistro table sat three and the delicate breeze that slipped in was refreshing as it ruffled the hot pink geraniums. The street below them was bustling with people running errands or just taking a leisurely walk.

"Any improvement with your Gran Chloe?" Glenda worried for her knowing just how fragile her past was and how important her Gran was to her. She unwrapped a large kaiser bun filled with assorted meats and cheeses, then took a big bite. Reaching for a napkin, she wiped off a dab of mayonnaise from her lip and then took another bite.

Chloe looked down at her boring garden salad despondently and set the fork down. "To be honest, I am not pleased at all with her progress. I actually am baffled to say the least.

I've been meaning to speak with her doctor, but it's been so hectic here. And when I'm back in Sarnia, I just want to visit with my Gran. I've been putting it off." She sighed and then reached for her water and sipped it as she waited for Glenda to respond. Her stomach grumbled and she wished that she would have been more creative with her lunch.

"Maybe some people take longer to recover from strokes. You mustn't blame yourself. I know that she wants to get better and she will. She is a tough cookie!" She leaned over to hug Chloe after setting the sandwich down on the small table.

"You're right. Thank you, Glenda. Love you."

"I love you too Chloe, more than you'll ever know." She smiled with tears in her eyes and pulled out a small box from her tote bag and handed it to her.

"For me?" Glenda nodded as she opened it and then squealed with delight. "A chocolate cupcake, thanks so much!" Discarding the salad, she dove enthusiastically into the confectionary, getting icing on her nose.

A Gran Scheme

Chloe made the anticipated call as she drove to see her Gran early Friday morning. She reached Dr. Nelson's voicemail and left him a message to call her at his earliest convenience. He returned her call just a half hour later while she was driving on the Highway 402 to Sarnia.

She answered via her Bluetooth. "Hello."

"Hi Chloe, this is Dr. Nelson." His voice was crisp.

"Thank you calling. I wanted to speak with you about my Gran and have some questions for you. Her progress has been slow and I have great concerns."

"Of course, but I am somewhat confused as she isn't my patient anymore. Have you discussed your concerns with her new doctor?" He seemed slightly aloof, almost agitated.

"I don't understand. What has happened? Why isn't my Gran in your care now?" Chloe was puzzled by his comment.

"Many months ago, during our telephone conversation, you explained that you were taking your Gran to Oakville. There, you would be continuing her rehabilitation with a new doctor as well as speech, physical and occupational therapists." He sounded somewhat exasperated.

Chloe gasped as he spoke. She felt as though she lost consciousness for a moment as her front tire caught some of the gravel, drawing the car off the road. She turned the wheel away from the shoulder with wide eyes and fear brewing inside of her. The gravel churned from her tires as she regained control of the car, forcing her attention back to driving. Her mouth was dry as she waited for an opportunity to pull over safely to the shoulder. Several cars passed before she maneuvered to the side, crunching through the stones. Her whole body shot forward as she put the car in park and covered her face with both hands.

"Chloe, are you there? Are you okay?" His voice was urgent as he waited impatiently for a response.

"Yes." It was a mere whisper croaked from her lips.

"Listen, I have a patient waiting. May I call you back later? I feel that we have much more to talk about."

A Gran Scheme

"I do want to speak with you further please." Chloe felt as though all of the oxygen had been removed from the air as she struggled to draw it into her lungs. She sat for a lengthy period as cars sped by, trying to absorb the conversation that she just had. She was numb as she called the office to let them know that she was taking a leave of absence. When she couldn't reach Glenda or Doc Benson, she left a message on his machine. Not wanting to cause them worry, she was vague with her information and would explain when she knew more. Chloe cried as she drove to her Gran's blaming herself for letting her down. She had failed her greatly by leaving to go back to work. Her eyes felt puffy from the tears she shed; her body exhausted. A wave of dizziness grasped her as she opened the car door, then realizing that she hadn't put it in park. All of it was like a bad dream that she couldn't escape from. Her poor Gran in the worse predicament of all. As she was reaching for her purse, her phone fell out onto the seat, but she didn't notice. Racing up the steps, she flung open the door and called out despairingly.

"Hi Chloe, we're all in the kitchen making snickerdoodles." June's voice sounded demonic to her now that she knew what kind of a person she really was. She walked down the hall, feeling like a zombie, barely blinking. She ran to her Gran and put her arms around her for dear life, silently crying.

"What's wrong?" June looked suspiciously at her as she took the cookies from the oven with large oven mitts on. Carl was sitting at the table sipping a cup of coffee looking uncomfortable as he cleared his throat, then coughed.

"I just spoke to Dr. Nelson June and he told me everything." Chloe stood up to confront her, looking her straight in the eye. June turned white as a sheet, before slowly taking off the oven mitts and answering.

"I don't know what you're talking about."

"I think that you do. My Gran has not had any sort of rehabilitation for a long time. You pretended to be me and told Dr. Nelson that she was moving to Oakville. Why would you do this?"

June's hand flew to her mouth in guilt, wishing that she would have left the oven mitts on and choked the living life out of her. "This is all a misunderstanding Chloe. You must believe that I would never do any of this. Layla means the world to me, to us. They have made a mistake, she has been attending her appointments, right Carl?" Her eyes squinted wickedly as she pointed to him for support. As he fumbled for words, she left the room hastily for a moment.

"Hmmm." He cleared his throat all the while perspiring as Chloe started to cry. She opened her purse and fumbled through it to find her phone. Realizing that it must have fallen out in the car, she went to her Gran's telephone to get help. But, before she could dial, June gave her an injection in her arm that caused her to pass out. The phone dangled by the cord, swinging. Carl helped put her on the living room sofa. She placed the phone back in the cradle spitefully while Layla watched horrified. The little dog lay quietly on her lap. Viciously, June took Iris and locked the little dog in the bathroom. *Now that pesty dog can go to the animal shelter,* she mused.

"Why did you go and do that for June? What are we going to do now?" Carl was wringing his hands aggressively over and over like a wet cloth. His mouth felt like sandpaper and each time that he swallowed, it abrased his tongue like a chunk of wood.

"Shut up Carl! I need you to put a lock on the door of the room in the basement and then we'll take Chloe down there. There is a bathroom with a shower as well." The small workshop was Winston's and he had loved to do woodworking and small projects there in his free time. He also put the washroom in so that he could clean up without getting sawdust all over the upstairs.

"This is considered kidnapping. I don't want to be apart of it." He stood tall. His voice was husky sounding and for once he didn't clear his throat.

"Really! Just do it. We're in this way too deep to give up now. Do you want to go to jail for a few years?" She sneered at him and grabbed a cookie off of the baking sheet. As she took a big bite, she noticed Layla watching and crying. She was also making a choking sound which annoyed June even more. Then, she raised herself from the chair and stood up wobblily with a fierce look on her face. Tossing the treat back onto the counter with disgust, June pushed her back down into the chair with zest. After giving her medication, she and Carl put her to bed to sleep.

Once back in the kitchen, she resumed eating her cookie without a plate as one hand rubbed her lower back. The crumbs encrusted her pursed lips like breading on chicken. The work was tedious. Layla required help to do almost everything and it was taking a toll on her. Of course, the medicine slowed down her progress, she could do a lot more without it. Never would June permit that to happen.

Within minutes Carl had fastened a metal latch on the outside of the small room in the basement with the adjacent washroom. Adept with his power tools, his handyman work was notable. He then moved the twin mattress from Chloe's bedroom upstairs and positioned it on the concrete floor against the wall. June bustled behind him carrying a pillow and some blankets, struggling to keep up. It was cool and dark without any windows for her to escape. Together, they moved Chloe carefully down the stairs with Carl taking her upper body and June her feet. She was still unconscious, her breathing labored. Layla had cleaned out the room decades ago and donated Winston's machinery to those who would value it so there was nothing that could be used to escape. They laid her down as June huffed and puffed with displeasure.

"I want you to pull Chloe's car into the garage and look for her cell phone." June gave the orders and he followed them like her slave.

Later, she brought down some supper for Chloe with Carl. She began to scream loudly when they unlocked the door.

"Settle down Chloe, or you'll miss eating tonight. And so will your Gran if you don't co-operate." She hissed the words with a vengeance like an army sergeant.

"Please let me out. I promise to do what ever you want. I just want to be with my Gran!" Her voice pleaded with them between sobs that caught deep in her throat garbling the words.

"Sit down on the mattress. We're going to open the door now so no funny business." Carl slid the latch over, cracked the door open and peered through the small opening. She was sitting on the bed as instructed so he put the plate on the floor with the water and then pushed it shut. Chloe ran to the door and threw her body on it just as he was sliding the latch across. She began to pound on it and shriek wildly.

"Remember what we said. Your sweet Gran will suffer severely if you don't stay calm and do as we say. If you act up, you will be sedated once more." June felt exhausted as she dragged herself upstairs by the handrail with Carl to eat.

The days went by painfully slow now as they lived in fear of being caught. Carl snuck books from Layla's massive collection down to Chloe for her to read. He put his finger on his lips to remind her not to say anything to June. Chloe placed them under the mattress on the cool floor. She was grateful to have something to read in the quiet basement as she was held captive. On Friday just before noon, there was a slight knock on the front door. Carl jumped as June glared at him and shook her head deliberately. She set her coffee mug down with a bang and gave Layla who sat staidly in her wheelchair a wicked look. Before she went to answer it, she and Carl hurried downstairs to warn Chloe about making any sort of a disturbance. Together they grabbed her as June roughly stuck a syringe into her arm. Within seconds, she passed out and they laid her down on the mattress, covering her mouth with a small piece of silver duct tape. After quickly wrapping both her ankles and wrists together with the same tape, both rushed back upstairs. The knocking had become more urgent.

Peering cautiously through the small window, she was relieved to see the familiar young lady standing there holding two large paper bags.

"Hi Chanel, what a pleasant surprise! Sorry, I took so long to answer the door, we were tending to Layla." She could feel her mouth watering as her nose met the delectable aroma.

"I'm sorry that I just dropped in, but I brought lunch for all of you. Fish and chips with coleslaw and tarter sauce. Oh, and ginger ales of course!" She smiled through a perfect set of white teeth and June returned hers; a crooked, yellow one.

"Why, that's just so nice of you! I'll just take it in for everyone to enjoy. Thank you." She reached out eagerly for the bags with her stubby hands but Chanel didn't let go. Her nails were painted a light glossy pink color and she wore a small butterfly ring on one of her fingers.

A Gran Scheme

"I was hoping to see Layla and Chloe for a little visit as well if that's okay." Her hair was shiny and her skin glowing with sheer loveliness and June resented her. Some women were just born that way and then others like her were cheated. She knew her mother as well and she was also a beauty.

June forced a rigid smile. "Of course, come in. Chloe is not here unfortunately but Layla will be overjoyed." The delicious aroma of the meal inside the paper bags teased her appetite and she couldn't wait to dive in. Without delay she set the table with plates and cutlery while Chanel visited with Layla.

"Layla, how are you? I brought you your favorite meal to enjoy. Too bad Chloe's not here. Hey, where is Iris?" Her head swung around so she could look around the kitchen for the sweet dog. Her long ponytail tied with a pink velvet ribbon danced in the air excitedly. Carl caught June's dirty look prompting him to exit the room quickly to return with her in his arms. She had made him lock the poor thing away and he wanted to keep her from June's repulsive behaviour anyway. He set her down and Iris ran directly to Chanel, waving her tail. She picked her up and gave her smooches before setting her on

Layla's lap. Taking a plate, she put a piece of fish and a nice portion of chips on it with a pair of tongs. As she added coleslaw and a dab of tarter sauce, June intervened.

"I'll do that Chanel. No need to bother yourself. And I'm sure that you have to get back to work. Your mother must need you there."

"Seriously. I don't mind and I'm on my lunch now anyways." She cut a small mouthful of fish, dipped it in the sauce and fed it to Layla. After she gave her a few mouthfuls, she opened a can of ginger ale, stuck in a straw and held it to Layla's lips as she drank. Good god, she was like a modern-day Florence Nightingale. June scrunched her face and rolled her eyes at the serenity of it all, causing her to look even more wicked.

"Is that good Layla?" June could take a pointer or two from her gentle mannerisms, Carl thought blatantly as he observed the compassionate scene. She gobbled up her fish and chip meal in just moments, looking greedily at Chloe's still in the bag. Layla enjoyed one piece of fish and most of her chips while June prayed silently for the *"lady with the lamp"* to go back to work.

A Gran Scheme

"Thanks again for thinking of us today. Everything was delicious. I'll just put Chloe's in the fridge and she can have it later when she gets back." June stood up briskly hoping to prompt her to leave. The sound of the chair squealed like a woman's high-pitched voice as it ran across the tiled flooring angrily, penetrating the eardrum.

"Sounds good. Okay, well goodbye Layla, I'll see you soon and you too Iris. Say hello to Chloe for me." She hugged them both and said her goodbyes to Carl and June as they rushed her to the door. June watched sneakily through the living room window until Chanel disappeared down the street and then hurried back to the kitchen. The lingering salt and vinegar aroma on her lips tickled her nostrils. Taking the crispy fish out of the box, she placed it on her plate, then dumped the fries beside it. June shoved several of the light, airy fries in her mouth as she slathered tarter sauce on the fish. Her fingers were shiny from the oil and she licked each one like a cat licking its paws after a saucer of fresh cream. She finished off not only Chloe's meal, but the rest of Layla's before wiping her mouth on the back of her sleeve and belching rudely. Carl looked repulsed at her.

"Well, what are you sitting there staring at Carl? Help clean up this mess and I'll take Layla to the washroom before her afternoon rest". She plucked Iris off her lap and plopped her down on the floor as she pretended to wipe her hands on her loose-fitting pants in disgust. "And, put this dog somewhere out of my sight."

He watched her wheel Layla out of the room with vigor. Then tidied up the remains of the meal so generously brought to them by Chanel and her family. Carl was stunned that June greedily ate the rest without bringing anything down to poor Chloe. After he wiped down the table, he picked up Iris and took her outside to the backyard watching her frolicking through the grass. Back inside, he noticed that June had gone upstairs so he crept into Layla's room and put Iris into bed with her. The small set of dog stairs that he bought for her worked beautifully allowing the tiny dog to get up and down without falling. Iris curled up against her master snugly for a rest and he presumed that June must have sedated Layla. She was snoring ever so softly with her mouth open peacefully. He closed the door quietly and went to the kitchen to prepare something for poor Chloe to eat. Carl knew that she loved her salads so he made her a spinach one with apples, cranberries and creamy goat cheese. He pulled out the leftover quiche from the refrigerator that June made the day before and lightly heated it up in the microwave. Just as he finished plating, June sauntered in with a look of scorn on her pudgy face.

"What's this?" She glared at him as he cleared his throat, trying to invoke the words that were stuck and couldn't be moved.

"It's for Chloe. She hasn't eaten and I thought that she would appreciate something nice. And, you ate the lunch that Chanel brought." He said it firmly hoping to raise some guilt from deep inside her cold heart.

"Well, she's not having the last piece of quiche, that was supposed to be for my dinner later." Her hands violently took the dish out of his hands and lifted the quiche back onto the pie plate. After licking her fingers, she covered it with plastic wrap and placed it back in the refrigerator.

"I can't believe you! Save it for yourself then. I hope that you choke to death on it." He put a soft buttered roll on the plate with the salad to compensate for the absence of the quiche.

"Come on, let's get this downstairs to her. She must be dying of hunger." Sarcastically June huffed and gave him a dirty look then. The door to the basement creaked as they opened it, as did the wooden steps that led down to it. Each one moaning with agony as both pairs of feet descended them. Chloe was lying in the same position as when they constrained her and she whimpered when they came in.

"We brought you lunch Chloe." Carl cleared his throat as he noticed the tears rimming her eyes. He gently removed the duct tape slowly from her mouth wincing as she cried out in pain.

"Just hurry up Carl. Cut it off her wrists and ankles, I want to go up and relax!" He did as he was told without trying to hurting her. June placed the tray with her food down on end of the mattress without care and turned to leave.

"I hope that you like the salad." He cleared his throat before following June like a loyal dog and once outside it, latched the door. Chloe massaged her tender wrists as she wept softly. The skin around her mouth stung from the duct tape and she sat staring at the food wondering if there was medication in it. Standing up somewhat unstable, she walked over to her grandpa's work bench and reached out to touch it with a shaky hand. Her fingers began to caress like it was a living thing instead of a lifeless, inanimate object. It was alive to her though, filled with so many wonderful memories. She loved when he patiently showed her how to make a small birdhouse and a tiny cradle for her dolls. Her nail stopped on the faded red paint that was splattered in one area and scratched the hard coating. She had wanted the birdhouse to be bright red and sunshine yellow. Through her tears, she saw something gleaming and when she bent down, a familiar wrapper came into view. Tickled, Chloe picked it up and put it to her nose recalling how she and her grandpa enjoyed the butterscotch candies as they worked. Though it didn't have any scent left, she could still recollect the sweet, buttery flavor of the sweets. *"Remember savor, don't bite it!"*

There used to be a tall stool with a padded seat for her to sit on while he animatedly demonstrated the work. She would sit contentedly as he explained the fine details sucking on the candy and then it would be her turn to try. Chloe covered her eyes with her hands thinking about the happier times and prayed silently for help. Removing her hands, she glanced around for any way to escape the area. There were no windows in the room or the bathroom for her to climb out unfortunately. As she dragged her feet sluggishly back to the mattress on the cool concrete, her stomach rumbled. Tucking the golden wrapper under her pillow safely, she then stared at the meal that they prepared for her. Reluctantly, she began to eat the salad examining it for any signs of tampering. Her fork poised before each bite rummaging through it like a buried treasure. She finished the fresh chewy sourdough roll and drank the water thirstily that they put with it. Reaching under the mattress, she withdrew anther book to read. This one was an Agatha Christie book title *Five Little Pigs* and she thought that it was highly appropriate for the situation that she was in, except there were just two. Opening the first page, she caught her breath. The inscription read:

"To my sweetheart Layla Happy Birthday! Forever yours Winston XOXO".

Her heart swelled with love remembering the beautiful relationship that they shared for many years. And how heartbroken everyone was when he passed away from the sudden heart attack. Soon she was fully absorbed in the reading, captivated by the brilliant writing. As Chloe turned each page craving to know what happened next, the author's mastermind was becoming more prominent. No wonder her Gran had always loved the murder mysteries!

Chapter 15

June began to panic when she saw the backlog of missed calls on Chloe's cell phone. A large majority were from Glenda as well as Doc Benson at her optometry office.

"We can't let these calls go unanswered for much longer Carl. She's going to have to talk to Glenda and smooth things over or it'll arouse suspicion." June looked frazzled for once as she set the snickerdoodle cookie down without even taking a bite, which was rare.

Carl cleared his throat and frowned at his unfamiliar wife. "Why don't we just end all of this right now. Surrender and pay the price, it's over."

June spat at him. "Over? We're going to do

this my way; do you hear me?" He nodded like a puppet with her hand up his back, stoned faced. She described the plan to him like a fugitive planning an espionage. When she was finally finished, he was pale and sweating profusely.

"I hope it works June. It sounds wicked to me. And if she says something to alert them, we're finished." He mopped his brow with an old handkerchief from his pocket and shoved it back inside.

June eyed him miserably. "It'll work, trust me." Together they went downstairs on a mission to see Chloe and to orchestrate June's mastermind plan. Once again, her wrists and ankles were bound with the evasive duct tape.

"I want you to speak with Glenda from the optometry office and tell her that everything's good. I wrote down what you're to say, nothing else or your Gran will be punished. She will have a terrible fall down these basement stairs, I promise you. Do you hear me?"

Chloe looked horrified. "Yes, I promise. But, please do not hurt my Gran. I'll do what ever you want." She began to sob incoherently and June raised her voice shrewdly penetrating the membranes of Carl's eardrums. He flinched as she spoke.

"Stop fussing! I am going to dial the number now and you will begin with what I wrote down. Nothing more!" Chloe composed herself and almost lost it when she heard Glenda's friendly voice on the speaker.

"Royal Eye Care, Glenda speaking."

"Hi Glenda, it's me Chloe. "She kept her voice calm, when she really wanted to shout for help.

"Thank goodness, we have been so worried about you. Are you okay?" One could easily read the concern and compassion in her voice.

Chloe read the script as instructed. "Yes, and I'm so sorry for not keeping you updated. My Gran had a minor fall and sprained her ankle so I have been terribly busy attending to her."

"Oh, no!" Glenda gasped. "How is she doing now?'

"She's is fine, on the mend so to speak." Chloe glanced wryly at June thinking that she would never use that expression.

A Gran Scheme

"Oh, good. Do you have plans to come back to the office soon? Doc and I miss you so much." June stared at her and shook her head sharply.

"Not at this point, sorry. I'll let you know soon though." She decided to risk speaking more. "I wanted to ask you to please make sure that Mrs. Pearl continues her medication and that she doesn't remain trapped without her glasses."

Glenda was confused, but something deep in the pit of her stomach told her to go with it. "Of course, dear, it was really nice to hear from you. I know you're busy with your Gran, but please try to keep in touch."

"Goodbye Glenda, I love you." She almost choked out the words.

"Love you too Chloe." June hung up briskly glaring at her with hatred in her eyes. She felt like smashing the phone on the concrete, but held herself back.

"How was that? I did what you asked. I want to see my Gran now! I need to know that she's okay." Her eyes pleaded with them like a young child demanding a lollipop. She was crying so hard that she began to hyperventilate, grasping for each breath.

"You'll see her when I say so." After giving her a shot in the arm to calm her down, Carl removed the duct tape and covered her up with the comforter to sleep.

"Stop fawning over her, like she's a child. I'm your wife, I deserve more." Every word she spat out was coated now with hatred. "I want you to go to the store for some groceries, there's a list upstairs." He followed her up while she panted like she had just run a marathon, stopping to catch her breath half way up. She had easily gained thirty pounds in a very short period of time and the strain that it put on her was evident. Wheezing heavily, she waddled to the kitchen to grab the list for Carl and then went to look in on Layla. She was still lying in bed with Iris at her side and June went to remove the small dog, placing her spitefully in the bathroom.

Hours after Carl left, June glanced at her watch again. What in the devil was taking him so long, she wondered? It was lunchtime and she was starving. There were additional ingredients that she needed before she could start the pasta dish. Fuming, she called his cell phone, ready to explode. It rang and rang without him answering and she became delirious with anger. Munching on the cookies to calm her hunger, she couldn't figure out where the heck he was.

Little did she know, that Carl was sitting in his car in the supermarket parking lot staring at the list. Each of the items scrawled out quickly on the notepaper with elegant roses on the bottom. The colorful array reminded him of Layla's beautiful gardens and he sighed heavily. June wasn't a rose, only a thorn in his side and to all who knew her. He unwillingly opened the door to get out and then slammed it shut with a vengeance. He could feel the blood pumping through every vein in his body and a sharp throbbing at his temples. His hands tore up the list and threw it to the floor in protest. Carl started the car and drove away stone faced with a purpose; he had enough.

Later, June heard a car come up the driveway. Storming to the front door, she swung it open and was stunned to see two gruff policemen who pushed their way inside. She could see the image of the emergency lights reflecting radiantly in the hallway mirror. Another one was pulling up with it's lights on and two more policemen got out of the vehicle and rushed up the steps. An ambulance was not far behind them.

"June Stewart?" She nodded with her mouth open, contemplating running away. But there was no where to run, she was trapped like a rat now. The tall, lanky officer began to read her rights as she was handcuffed briskly and led outside to the police car. With the officer's hand on the top of her head, she was guided inside. She couldn't believe her eyes. That traitor of a husband of hers had turned himself in and threw her under the bus as well. Frightened, she watched horrified as the car backed down the driveway and sped down the road. Back inside, the other policemen ran downstairs to rescue Chloe who began to pound heavily on the door when she heard them calling out to her.

"Stand back from the door please, we're going to cut off the lock!" After a few moments, the door swung open and Chloe ran to them tearfully.

"My Gran, she's upstairs. I have to get to her." It felt like a nightmare that she could never imagine happening to her. Or her poor Gran.

A Gran Scheme

"She is safe. Come, I'll take you to her. Are you hurt?" Shaking her head no, she went with him. He was sympathetic as he helped her upstairs. The sunlight from the hallway slapped her eyes like a wet towel and she shielded them for a moment. Through vision that had not seen natural light in days, she forged on bravely to be with her Gran. The officer had helped her to sit up in bed with a few pillows behind her back.

"Gran! Oh, it's so good to see you again. I am so sorry for everything. I feel that I caused all of this misery for you and I will never forgive myself." She clung to her, relieved that it hadn't ended badly for either of them.

"Chloe." It was merely a whisper, but she heard it and started to cry harder.

"I love you Gran. Don't worry, I am going to get you the best care now for you to get better." She rested her head against her Gran's and stroked her back gently. After a few minutes, she heard a barking and stood up alarmed. "Iris? Where are you sweetie?" The whining led her to the bathroom where Iris leapt into her arms when she bent down to pick her up. Kissing her head, she placed the sweet dog beside her Gran on the bed. Iris wagged her tail animatedly with love and licked her hand as she smiled.

"How did you find us officer?"

"Well, it was a series of events actually. The first was when a Carl Stewart walked into the police station and surrendered himself. He told us everything, all of the despicable things that he and June did over the years. Not only to you and your Gran, but to the deceased Anna Wagner as well. Then, an urgent call came in almost at the same time from a Glenda at Royal Eye Care who said that something suspicious was going on there."

Chloe smiled. "I knew that she would figure out that we needed help. I gave her some subtle hints when we spoke that we were not okay and it worked." She remembered the murder mystery books that she read while being held captive, not knowing how much they would actually help. The paramedics examined both for any signs of medical distress or injuries.

"We would like for the ambulance to take your Gran to the hospital for further examination. And you as well. You are free to follow us in your vehicle. It is obvious that both of you were drugged numerous times and blood samples are imperative to the arrest and trial of the suspects." The officer, stated kindly. Although Chloe didn't want anymore inconvenience or evasive testing, she knew that he was right.

"Yes, officer, my Gran and I will go. I'll drive my Gran's SUV there so we'll have transportation back home." She had no idea as to where her purse, keys or phone was now. "I would like to take my purse if I can find it, my health card as well as keys are in it." She looked helplessly at each of them.

"Come, we'll help you look for it." After describing it to them, they found it in June's room with her cell phone. Noting all of the missed calls, she made a call quickly to her practice.

"Royal Eye Care, Glenda speaking." Her voice sounded strained, anxious.

"It's me Chloe."

"Are you alright? Your Gran? We have been overcome with worry so I called the police."

"Yes, we're both fine now, getting some medical attention. Thank you, Glenda, for calling them. You helped to save both of our lives. June and Carl were keeping Gran from getting better and they kidnapped me. I was locked in the basement." Chloe started to cry.

Glenda's voice quivered. "Oh, no! I can't believe how cruel they both are. It's unfathomable! Try not to think about it right now. We have been so worried and can talk more later. Doc and I want to come down tomorrow to see you both, to offer our support."

"Thank you, we would love the company right now. And we're both still frightened after what happened."

"See you soon. Love you and so glad that you're both fine!"

The staff at the hospital were patient and kind which put their minds at ease. The examination took several hours and they asked if Layla wanted to stay there overnight, but Chloe shook her head.

Her face was pleading. "If it's okay with you, I would rather take her home and make her as comfortable as possible. She has been through so much."

The doctor smiled and nodded. "Of course. You both have been through so much and I do want the best situation. I'll request help to assist you with transporting your Gran into your vehicle. If you need anything else, please just reach out to us." He touched Chloe's arm gently in a fatherly way.

"Thank you doctor." Chloe pushed her Gran down the long, sterile hallway and to the front lobby. There were several patients waiting to go home also, come with casts or bandages on. Within minutes, two hospital attendants arrived and waited with Layla until she brought the vehicle up to the front entrance. She stood up with some help and walked shakily to the door that Chloe opened for her. The attendants helped her inside and Chloe fastened the seatbelt for her. After the wheelchair was folded and placed in the back trunk area, they thanked them and were on their way home. She felt apprehensive as she drove up the driveway, like the house was haunted or cursed now. But it was her Gran's beloved house and she shook those thoughts from her mind. There were police and forensic vehicles at Anna's home which didn't help either. The officers had removed all of June and Carl's items as well as any evidence left there after receiving permission from her Gran. Neither wished to see anything affiliated with them upon returning home. They were also very kind to have the mattress from the basement taken away as well so she didn't have to see it. She preferred to order a new one for her bedroom.

Iris greeted them happily, tail wagging as soon as they walked in the door. Chloe made her Gran comfortable on the sofa and prepared a pot of camomile tea after feeding the little dog and taking her outside. She reached for the old-fashioned stovetop kettle that whistled when the water boiled and smiled. Stainless steel with an ornate handle, it was the one that she remembered her Gran using as a child. After filling it with water, she noticed the baking sheets on top of the stove. A subtle odour of prior baking still hung in the air, but could not be called inviting. Much similar to a skunk, penetrating the nostrils with an unwelcome odour. The putrid smell her like a punch in the stomach, causing her to suck in her breath. The snickerdoodle cookies that June had baked earlier and would most likely eat all of, were mocking her. Purposely, she walked over to the stovetop and lifted the trays, dumping each one into the trash can remembering the lemonade. *Freshly squeezed*, my eye she scoffed. June had lied about almost everything.

Chloe cleaned the cookie sheets and then she placed the kettle on to boil. How dare she do this to them, she stewed! And then bake cookies from their old family recipe as if she had no care in the world? Grandma Annette would roll over in her grave. Flat like overdone pancakes, she attributed it to using too much butter. An empty box of shortening infuriated her even more as she realized that the most important ingredient was altered. No wonder they didn't taste anything like the recipe. The piercing sound of the kettle whistling brought her back to the task at hand. After throwing the package out, Chloe shook her head in disgust and resumed making the tea. She put on a brave smile when she returned carrying the tray and sat beside her Gran. Iris relaxed cozily on her other side. As she poured the hot liquid from the fancy pot into the delicate teacups and added the honey, she heard three words.

"Thank you, Chloe." Layla smiled at her. The most beautiful lopsided smile in the world. Her left hand lifted and rested on Chloe's.

Chloe covered her hand with the other. "You're welcome, Gran." Lovingly she helped her to take a sip of tea.

On Saturday morning as promised, Doc Benson arrived with Glenda. They were in shock after hearing the entire story and deeply horrified. Chloe made them comfortable in the spare rooms and was grateful for the company. They stayed until Sunday morning and then left to go back to Oakville.

On top of her Gran's appointments, Chloe was also busy getting her home back in order. She scrubbed, polished and cleaned everything as if to remove any trace of the misery that she and her Gran suffered. As she was changing the sheets, her hand touched something hard under the mattress. Pulling it out, she was astonished to see the writing board that was supposedly "missing." June must have hidden it under there to prevent her Gran from writing anything. A wave of fresh guilt washed over her. It was all her fault for agreeing to go back to work. When June prompted her, she assumed it was out of compassion and not malice. Maybe none of this would have happened if she had been there to watch. Chloe couldn't change any of that now unfortunately.

When she finished the bedding, she forced herself go to the basement. She wanted the books that were still down there. She swallowed as she clung to the railing, her head dizzy. Slowly, she made her way down, barely breathing. Digging her nails into the palms of her hands, she turned on the light, then pushed open the door to the old workshop area. Her heart was pounding like a jackhammer as she swiftly picked up the books and ran back upstairs. Kneeling down in front of her Gran who sat comfortably in a reclining chair, she beamed. Then she opened the Agatha Christie book titled *Five Little Pigs* and showed her Gran the inscription.

Smiling, she spoke softly. "I remember. My Winston." The words were broken, but she understood her Gran.

"I read it twice while I was held captive. I think that I learned a thing or two from Agatha Christie! She is brilliant." Chloe hugged her and placed the book on top of her bureau.

"Bedroom. Upstairs. Box." Raising her left hand, her finger pointed upstairs.

"I don't understand Gran. What would you like me to help with?" She was puzzled.

"Open chest. Blue blanket. Go" She was determined and adamant that Chloe do as she asked.

"Okay, I'll be right back." She ran upstairs to her Gran's old bedroom and walked purposely to the beautiful antique chest at the end of the bed. Kneeling down and then taking a deep breath, she opened it. She saw the light blue banket on top of her Gran's keepsakes. Teary eyed, she caressed it with her hand, feeling the softness and knowing what it signified. The pain and suffering of losing a precious baby. Cautiously, she unfolded it. Wrapped inside was a letter which she placed on the floor and then refolded the beloved blanket. Glancing inside, she saw the countless drawings that she made for her Gran of she and her family. Seashells that they collected together and numerous small boxes underneath filled with special mementos. Her heart was in her throat as she closed the heavy lid down and picked up the envelope. Racing downstairs with it in her hand like a child back to her Gran.

"Here it is! The letter. Is this what you wanted me to bring down?"

She nodded. "Open." Chloe saw that it was addressed to Ms. Anna Wagner and pulled out the letter. After reading the first few lines, she gasped.

"Oh, no! That's why she never heard from him for months and months. Her son Felix died and she didn't even know it. They are true beasts. June and Carl deserve to be locked up for life. Why would they keep this from her?" Chloe was shocked beyond belief. "Poor, poor Anna. She would have been so heartbroken. I guess they are both resting together in Sweden now?"

Gran shook her head as furiously as she could. "No! Cremated. Anna's house." Tears sprang to her eyes as she sobbed for her dear friend.

"I am going to call the police station now and tell them about the letter and what you know." The policeman whose introduced himself as Officer Kent arrived shortly and they welcomed him into the kitchen. He took the letter for evidence and then explained to them what he could.

"Both Anna Wagner and her son Felix were cremated. Their ashes are in boxes and were found in the front hallway closet of the

Wagner home. Carl Stewart confessed that June took the call on the day that Felix Wagner died, impersonating his mother, Anna. She requested that his body be cremated and sent back to her as soon as possible. Then, when Anna passed away of cancer, Carl impersonated her son Felix, again requesting cremation."

"This is shocking to learn. And so sad." Chloe was crying freely now.

Officer Kent shook his head sadly. "Yes, Layla must have seen the letter as well as their ashes in the closet. It was when she saw June wearing Anna's prized ring that she had the stroke. And that's only the half of it. It would appear that they also altered the wills to leave them as sole beneficiaries to hers and Felix's estates. Carl admitted to stealing the valuables as well. And he confirmed that they began drugging Layla after her stroke so she wouldn't turn them in. A lawyer should also be in contact with you soon, Layla."

"But why officer Kent?" Chloe was confused.

"I am not at liberty to discuss the details yet, but soon you will know the rest." He left shortly afterwards and Chloe and her Gran sat together quietly mourning the information that they had just received. She had no idea the burden that her Gran carried around with her while battling her recovery. Those disturbing discoveries had most likely caused her stroke and could have killed her.

They heard from the lawyer a few days later and discovered that Layla, not June was named the true sole beneficiary if Felix was predeceased by his mother. Touched by her dear friend's generosity, she first wanted to give both Anna and her son a dignified burial. And then donate to the charities dear to Anna and her son Felix's hearts. The home would have to be sold as well. She knew that her dying wish was to be buried next to her husband Jordan. Her son would also be buried beside them. With Chloe's help, she made the arrangements with the funeral home to have a small service at the cemetery. It was a lovely September afternoon with just a handful of Anna's close friends and neighbors gathered to honor her memory. The leaves were just beginning to transform into the warm seasonal colors of fall. Crisp, cooler nights teased what was to come but the days still clung fiercely to the warmth of summer. When the service finished, they thanked everyone personally for showing their love and support.

"Such a nice service for our dear Anna and her son. Both can rest peacefully now beside her beloved husband." Ethel pursed her lips and tapped at her eyes with a worn, lace handkerchief.

"Yes. Thank you for coming, Ethel. Will Layla see you tomorrow at the Community Centre?" Chloe spoke for her Gran, who was still regaining her ability to speak clearly. Layla would begin by going once a week to sit with her friends and was eager to continue her activities there, especially swimming.

"Of course, we are all excited for you to be a part of the group again. See you tomorrow Layla and bye Chloe!"

Slowly, she and her Gran walked to the other side of the small cemetery to visit with their loved ones. The walker moved at a steady pace as her Gran pushed it skilfully. It still pierced her heart and took her breath away to see so many of their family members buried there. Her hand caressed the locket around her neck mournfully; there would always be a huge piece of her heart missing.

Chapter 16

Layla resumed her therapy and rehabilitation right away. It wasn't long before she was forming sentences with little effort and swimming again using flotation devices. Her facial drooping improved enormously as well. She had loathed the wheelchair and was happy for it to be finally gone. They had spent the last lazy days of summer relaxing together at the beach and reaping the rewards of her garden. Chloe beamed as they picked the tomatoes, peppers, squash and zucchini together as Iris lay watching in the grass under the sunshine.

Late September, they took their first major walk down the street to get chips under the bridge and Layla did magnificently. Smiling the whole way, she proved that she was a true warrior as she pushed her walker.

"Layla, Chloe! How nice to see you. Have a seat, lunch is on us." Chanel and her mother Alana were delighted to see them. By now, everyone in the area had heard about their ordeal. Alana thought that it was heartbreaking after everything else they had been through.

"That's so kind. And, thank you Chanel for bringing lunch that day. So very sweet of you to think of my Gran and myself." Chloe gave her a hug and sat down at the table.

"If only I had known that something was up. I would have called the police on those two beasts." She frowned like she did something wrong. Her father Chris and brother Calvin waved from the kitchen.

"No, please don't think that way. You had no idea what monsters they were. None of us did until the end." Alana brought the fish and chips out herself with two cans of ginger ale. Her loveliness shone even at her age, and it was obvious as to where her daughter inherited her beauty from.

"I'm so glad that you two are doing well. Here it is, happy eating!"

"Thank you!" Layla beamed at them both and Alana hugged her. She went back into the kitchen while Chanel continued to wipe tables and tidy up the eatery.

Chloe's Gran continued to improve and amaze her doctors and therapists alike. Now using just a cane, Layla was able to complete minor tasks around her home and prepare simple meals. One rainy October afternoon, her Gran said. "Let's bake some snickerdoodle cookies."

Chloe shuddered as she remembered June baking them. "I don't think that I can, Gran. They make me think of all the bad stuff that happened to us."

"We must put that behind us now and great grandma Annette would turn over in her grave if we didn't pay homage to her recipe ever again!" She reached out to touch Chloe's arm tenderly as Iris danced around the kitchen and barked.

"Okay, let's do it! We'll eat them warm with a cup of tea." She put on the radio, smiling as one of the older classic songs came on. Her Gran began to sing along in her harmonic voice as Chloe gathered up the ingredients. Reaching for the butter, she was then reminded of the shortening that June had substituted instead. Pushing that farthest from her mind, she sang along with her Gran as they made the delicious family recipe. The beater sang as it whipped the butter in the mixing bowl until it was light and fluffy. Chloe added the eggs and vanilla. Just before they were to be rolled in the cinnamon sugar, Gran made a suggestion.

"What do you think about adding one extra ingredient to the recipe?" Gran had a twinkle in her eyes.

Pretending to be shocked, Chloe replied. "What! Tamper with perfection? Tell me."

"White chocolate chunks! I think that Grandma Annette would approve."

"Sounds so good! I'll chop the chocolate. I cannot wait to try them." Chloe hummed to the music, then she and her Gran danced to some songs as the cookies were baking. The aromatic scent of cinnamon was magical. She put the kettle on while they were cooling and then placed some of the warm snickerdoodles on a plate to go with their tea.

"Wow! These sure are delicious! The white chocolate was such a nice idea Gran. Yum!" Chloe looked like a young child again as she ate them hungrily and sipped her tea. It reminded Layla of when she visited on the weekends and in the summer years ago. It melted her heart whenever she thought of those days, when they spent valuable time together making memories. And she felt blessed that they still shared prized time to the very day.

Layla listed Anna's house with a real estate agent and it sold just weeks later. Layla met with Lena and Taylor Hall and the agent when they put in the offer and immediately felt at ease. She knew that they would love and cherish Anna's home as promised. The children, five-year-old Jade and eight-year-old Miles were well mannered and their parents extremely pleasant. The agent had generously helped Chloe box up the remainder of Anna's belongings and transported them to her Gran's basement with the help of his oldest son. Inside, the photographs that she cherished and some personal items. Layla donated her clothing and most of the other housewares, but didn't have the heart to throw anything out. Many of the other insignificant items had been disposed of by June and Carl when they took over the home. And the new owners wanted to keep all of the furniture, which was a blessing. Layla's antique chest from her old bedroom upstairs was also brought down and placed at the end of her bed as she wished.

With December, came snow, masses of it and then Christmas. It was a tender time of year for them. They celebrated it together with a real fir tree, which they decorated with Layla's treasured keepsake ornaments. After a traditional breakfast of fluffy pancakes, they went to the Christmas morning service before exchanging gifts by the tree. Layla now walked without a cane or walker and had astounded the doctors with her miraculous recovery.

"This is for you Gran; I hope that you like it." The large box was wrapped with care and she opened it without any help from Chloe. Lights from the tree twinkled behind her like a million stars, casting an angelic glow around her head.

Layla gasped. "Is this one of those digital photo frames?"

"Yes, let me show you how it works." Layla followed her to her bedroom where she placed it on the bureau and then plugged it into an outlet. Right away, a special photograph of Chloe and her Gran appeared on the screen for a short time before making way for the next one. She watched with teary eyes as each of the sentimental photographs displayed, even ones of her and Winston. There were several family ones that she had forgotten about and she broke down when Arabella, Grayson, Ariana and Chloe appeared on the screen smiling happily. Taken just before the tragedy, it was the last family photograph of them with their family dog. "I didn't mean to make you sad Gran." There were tears of heartbreak in her eyes a well.

"I truly love it, Chloe. Everyone that I cherish is preciously held in a frame for me to be close to each day. Thank you, it is a very touching gift, I'll treasure it always. And this is for you." Layla dabbed at her eyes as she handed Chloe the white envelope with a glimmer in her eye.

Baffled, she took the envelope. "What's this Gran?" Her hand held it like a piece of fragile glass as her fingers caressed the exterior.

"Open it and see silly! It won't bite you." She had orchestrated the whole thing with the help of Doc Benson and Glenda. Chloe opened it gingerly and stared at the letter inside while she held the ticket.

"I'm going to the Canadian Association of Optometrist's Congress in Halifax, Nova Scotia?" Her eyes were wide with fear.

Layla laughed. "Don't look so happy about it! You have always wanted to go but keep pushing it off every year. And, I hear that July is a beautiful time to go."

"But I can't go and leave you alone Gran."

"It's months away and I am becoming more independent each and every day. It will be fine, you'll see." She hugged her granddaughter then for dear life.

Later that evening, Lena and Taylor came over with the children for Christmas cookies and hot apple cider. Miles made a beautiful pine comb ornament for the tree and Jade painted a picture for them. Chloe and her Gran gave them gifts, a doll for Jade and Lego for Miles as well as a small bag of chocolate Santas each. They played some popular board games around the kitchen table and the house felt alive again with the chatter and laughter of little ones. It was truly a memorable Christmas and the heartache that they recently experienced seemed miles away.

Chloe and her Gran rang in the New Year hours before because neither could stay up to midnight to ring in the toast. The night was enchanting as they ate delicious food and played cards. Armed with a glass of Champagne, they clanged their flutes and made a New Year's resolution before turning in.

In early spring, Layla was given the privilege of driving again which boosted her morale immensely. She took her first drive to the community centre to swim and afterwards to the library. She unwrapped a butterscotch candy from her purse and eagerly pressed it onto her tongue. It was pleasurable for her to just sit with her eyes closed and imagine the days when she was younger. She still blushed at the thought of Winston sitting at his desk with the jar of golden wrapped candies. And how her heart raced when he offered her one. The buttery flavor warmed her heart and she could almost feel his presence beside her. Smiling, she remembered how infatuated she was with him and still was to this day.

"Hi Layla. How are you?" The rich voice brought her back to the present and her eyes fluttered open. Her friend Ethel from the community centre was standing over her with a handful of books in her arms. She wore a red wool coat that fought viciously with her bright red hair and glossy lips.

"I'm well, thank you. You look wonderful!" She had began having her hair dyed to impress a gentleman at the centre that she had a crush on. It made her feel like a teenager again.

Her hand coiffed her hair and she giggled. "The things we do for a man's interest." They spoke for a few moments longer before Ethel checked her books out, then Layla chose a few to read. Driving was like riding a bike and she felt very comfortable as she maneuvered the car up her driveway and into the garage when she reached home. The real estate agent had recommended a reputable landscape company to take care of her property and the snow was always cleared first thing. Layla was highly anticipating the early blooms that would pop up soon. Chloe greeted her at the front door and looked relieved when she arrived home in once piece.

A Gran Scheme

"Well, how did it go Gran? Your first day of full independence!" Chloe had almost chewed her fingernails off waiting for her Gran to return.

"It went very well dear. I thoroughly enjoyed my swim and visit to the library. How did you do without your old Gran here?" She smiled lovingly at her and wished secretly that she wouldn't worry so much about her. It bothered her that her granddaughter had put her whole life on hold to be with her.

Chloe grinned. "Apart from worrying about you the whole time, fine. I made us a big pot of minestrone soup for dinner." Layla laughed and hugged her as she reached for the bag, she was carrying full of books. "I see that you have acquired some more reading material. Anything interesting?"

"Actually, there were some new mystery writers that I decided to try. I'll let you know which ones that I like best, if you'd like to read them as well."

"Yes, I'd like that." Chloe ladled the hearty soup into her Gran's porcelain bowls that matched the other dainty China set while Layla sliced the sourdough bread into thick slices for dipping.

"It smells wonderful and I have worked up quite an appetite! Thank you, Chloe."

"You're very welcome. Hope you like it." They settled down for a movie afterwards that made them both laugh and cry almost at the same time. Chloe woke up the next day to the smell of bacon sizzling and stretched for a few moments before getting out of bed. The air felt slightly cool and she could feel the warmth radiating from the furnace through the vents in the floor. She stuck her feet into the cozy slippers on the floor by her bed. Grabbing a sweatshirt from the hook on her bedroom door, she pulled it on as she sashayed downstairs following the succulent aroma.

"Good morning sleepyhead!" Gran stood fully dressed in a pair of slacks and cashmere sweater as she cooked scrambled eggs in a large frying pan. On the countertop were two plates garnished with sliced tomatoes and old cheddar cheese.

Breathing the delicious air in Chloe hugged her. "Good morning. Breakfast smells heavenly! Is there anything that I can do?" It seemed like her Gran had thought of it all. A pot of tea sat on the table accompanied by cream and honey. There was even a plate with small ramekins filled with condiments such as ketchup and salsa verdi.

"Sit and enjoy." After they finished eating and tidying up the kitchen, her Gran asked if they could have a little talk in the living room. Each sat comfortably on the sofa with a fresh cup of tea before she began.

"Chloe, I think it's time for you to return to work." Flabbergasted, Chloe started to object but Layla held up her hand to finish. "Please listen even though you may not like what I'm about to say. You have given up a career and lifestyle that you adore to be here for me. And, I couldn't love you more for it or be more grateful for such a wonderful and loving granddaughter. But I cannot take you time up any longer, day by day your sacrifice for me. I am now able to take care of myself and my desire is for you to fulfill your days doing something that you love. Do you understand what I'm saying?" Her eyes showed her more love than she had ever felt in her entire life and she nodded slowly.

"Yes, I just feel as though I'm abandoning you like before when I went back to work and the unthinkable happened. I still blame myself for all of it." Chloe started to cry, oceans of pent-up tears that she kept bottled up inside and Layla held her. When she was finished, she nodded. "I will do as you wish Gran."

"That's my girl! And you know how lovely Lena and Taylor are next door. They are always checking in and the children are such a joy! You have nothing to worry about now." She winked at her and took Chloe's hand in hers and she could feel the warmth to her soul. One would never guess that Layla had ever had a stroke, her recovery was nothing short of astonishing.

Doc Benson and Glenda were overjoyed when they heard that she would be resuming her work at the office soon. Glenda didn't want to alarm her, but Doc was working 10-hour days without her there. Nor, was he able to have much time off, if any. They chatted more about the upcoming Canadian Association of Optometrist's Congress in Halifax, Nova Scotia in July before hanging up. Chloe would be going back to her home in Oakville after many months and it felt strange. Apart from checking her house bi-weekly and sorting the mail, she hadn't stayed nor slept there in so long.

A Gran Scheme

The day of Chloe's departure was sheer agony for them both, even though her Gran didn't show it. Their last dinner together was celebrated with fish and chips under the bridge. Chanel, Calvin and their mother Alana sat with them. Afterwards, all celebrated Chloe's goodbye with huge ice cream sundaes topped with whipped cream and a cherry.

"Promise, you'll call me if you feel sad or lonely Gran?" Chloe's eyes were big and round with despair as she spoke.

"Of course, I promise. And you do the same, okay?" Layla's face was brave, but if one looked closely, there were tears forming in her eyes. They hugged one last time before Chloe got into her car and reluctantly drove off. She felt even worse than the last time that she left, like she would never see her Gran again. She would rather have all of the teeth in her mouth pulled than feel like this. She had to stop herself from crying because her eyes were so clouded over that she couldn't see to drive. The trip home seemed endless and the farther she drove away from Sarnia, the more desolate she felt.

Relieved when she finally saw the Oakville sign, she maneuvered the car off of the highway and to her home. This time, instead of leaving her car in the driveway, she pressed the garage door opener and pulled it into her garage. Something that she was always too frightened to do even with her electric car. Being in the garage reminded her of the horrible fate that met her family years ago, but now she had to overcome it. After removing her baggage from the trunk, she carried it inside and set it down in the mudroom to unpack later. She helped herself to a glass of wine and then called her Gran quickly to let her know she had arrived home safely. Chloe unpacked her suitcases, cleaned the house and put in a load of laundry before peering in the refrigerator for something to eat. Other than a few condiments and sour milk that she poured down the drain, it was bare. She looked in the cupboards and when that proved fruitless, she pulled a frozen margherita pizza from the freezer and popped into the oven. She poured another glass of wine while she ate the pizza and watched the evening news. Of course, her crush, Zane Remington was on and she laughed thinking that some things never change. Then a frown washed over her face when she thought about everything that was so different now. The inside of her shiny locket was a constant reminder of that. She took a quick trip to the supermarket after making a list of groceries, purchasing the necessities as well as some additional indulgences that she saw.

When Monday rolled around, Chloe was up early and eager to see her patients again. She applied a subtle hint of makeup and brushed her hair until it shone past her shoulders. Dressed in a navy skirt and ruffled blouse, she made her coffee to go and drove to the office. Glenda looked up when she walked in and gleefully ran over to hug her.

"Welcome back Chloe. We missed you so much!" Doc Benson moseyed out when he heard the commotion with a big grin on his face.

"Well, look at what the cat dragged in! So glad that you're back." His eyes were moist as he embraced her warmly.

Chloe felt more at ease. "Thanks, it's really nice to be here. Have I missed much?" She felt guilty that she left Doc Benson holding the bag for months, but there was no other choice for her.

"Come and sit in my office, I'll fill you in." By mid afternoon, Chloe was back in the game again and feeling confident. Her patients greeted her lovingly and she felt valued. Truly, she loved her profession and couldn't dream of doing anything else. Her Gran was right and when she got home later that night, she called her happily with a big grin on her face.

"Chloe, how did your day go?" Layla's eyes twinkled as she listened, she could see how happy she was.

"Wonderful, Gran! It felt so good to be working again and helping others. My day just sped by!"

"I'm delighted to hear that. You're extremely good at what you do and I bet your patients were thrilled to see you!" Layla had spent the day keeping busy so she wouldn't miss her dear granddaughter terribly. She met her friends at the community centre for coffee and cards in the morning, then went to the market before returning home to take Iris for a walk.

"Thank you! And yes, everyone was so nice." They continued talking for a few more minutes, then said their goodbyes after her Gran put Iris on to say *hello!*"

A Gran Scheme

It was on Friday that Doc Benson asked to speak with her in his office. Chloe hoped that her first week back was a success. He looked serious as she walked in after knocking on his door.

"Hi, am I in trouble Doc?" She was only half joking and he saw that she was nervous.

"Not at all. The opposite in fact. What a successful week for you. And so many happy patients. If you hadn't caught Mrs. Wrights Diabetic Retinopathy, it may have gone on further causing her total vision loss. Great job Chloe!" Alicia Wright was new to their practice and referred to them by a prestigious colleague of his.

Chloe breathed a sigh of relief. "Thank you. I'm glad that I went ahead and ordered the testing to be sure. When the tests came back indicating Diabetic Retinopathy, I then referred her to a doctor and discussed treatment options with her." She looked proud of herself as she spoke.

"Excellent "eye" Chloe!" He laughed as did she at his pun. "Now, I want to talk about something else before your head gets too big. As you know, I'm not young anymore and retirement is looking extremely attractive right now. Marie wants us to travel and just enjoy each other's company now."

Stunned, Chloe spoke gently. "So, when will you be leaving? Have you set a date?" Her right hand was holding the locket around her neck for comfort.

"I would like to say the middle of June, if we can find a suitable partner in time." It was the beginning of May. "Of, course I will continue to help and train the new candidate for as long as required. There has been a good amount of interest and I have narrowed it down to four of which I feel have great potential." His face showed signs of fatigue and she felt sorry for him. She would be forever grateful for everything that he did for her. Especially saving her mother's office for her.

"I understand Doc. And I'm happy for you and Marie, you both deserve it so much!" She let go of the locket and got up with tears in her eyes to give him a hug.

"Now, I'm relieved. Whew, this was difficult for me to say, especially with the suffering that you and your Gran just went though. But I want you to know that I'm not deserting you or the practice. I'll be here for as long as you need me." The amount of pain that they endured over the years was upsetting.

"I know." Chloe smiled even though she was still digesting the news. It wouldn't be the same with him gone. Frightened she hoped that Glenda wouldn't leave her too.

He held up a file. "Take this folder of applicants to read. All have great attributes and would be an asset to the office. Ultimately, the final choice is up to you. Goodnight Chloe, have a relaxing weekend." He gave her a firm hug.

"You as well Doc. Tell Marie that I say *hi*." Afterwards, Chloe sat at her mother's antique desk poring over the potential partners chuckling at Doc's notes on each of them. Two were women and two were men and as he mentioned, all were impressive. There were extra notes on one which she read carefully, then glanced at the top to see the name Ollie. Doc described him as compassionate and outgoing with a good sense of humor. Chloe giggled again, of course that would be on the top of Doc's list of attributes. She saw that he held a major in ocular disease and worked with clinical professors treating glaucoma and co-managing cataract, oculoplastic and retinal disease patients. Ollie was also involved in presenting continuing education lectures which was commendable. He was currently involved in a multinational study for diabetic retinopathy with a leading research hospital in Toronto. She whistled. No wonder Doc was fascinated with his application. Chloe put the file down on her desk and after completing a few more tasks, she prepared to leave for the weekend. On Monday, she would have Glenda set up the interviews and go from there. After putting on her light coat, she went to speak with Glenda.

"I can't believe that Doc Benson is retiring, I am still in shock!"

Glenda finished typing and stood up to talk. "Shocking is right, I thought that he would work until he was ninety! He does deserve it though."

"Yes, he sure does. I hope that I can run things as good as he did all of these years. The patients love him also." Chloe's eyes held the kind of pain that most would never experience in their entire lives luckily. If you looked into them deeply, it was haunting. Glenda always felt the urge to mother her.

"You're going to be wonderful! Time now to enjoy the weekend. Are you going to visit your Gran?"

The pain in her eyes turned to sheer joy. "Yes, I'm leaving first thing in the morning and will be back Sunday evening. I cannot wait. Do you have plans with your grandchildren?"

"Yes, we are taking them to the African Lion Safari on Sunday. I think that they are going to love it!" Glenda looked just as excited as the children would be.

Laughing, Chloe agreed. "That will be loads of fun. Have a great time, okay!" The spring air was still warm when she walked to her car and she inhaled deeply. The tulips and daffodil planters were a delight to the senses and she could smell the perfumed scent of the hyacinths. She drove her car into the garage when she reached home and walked up to the mailbox to extract her mail. It felt good to kick off her pumps and swathe her feet in the cozy slippers. She wasn't used to wearing them all day and she relished the thought of an evening of relaxation before traveling in the morning.

Chloe's visit with her Gran was simply the best. They took long walks with Iris, sat by the water observing the boats and relishing in their favorite meal of fish and freshly made chips. It was just like old times and they both were thankful for the warmth of spring after a cold, harsh winter in many ways. The weekend was over much too fast, hence ending her visit with her Gran, but this time she knew that everything would be alright.

The interviews for Chloe's new associate were arranged by Glenda for Thursday with two in the morning and the remainder in the afternoon. The first ones went well, but there was something absent. After lunch, the next candidate arrived and the interview went smoothly, but there was no spark. She started to get nervous. What if she couldn't choose any of them? Sweat began to form at the back of her neck under her hair as she panicked. The buzzing of the telephone told her that the last candidate had arrived.

"Send him in please Glenda." Chloe quickly blotted her neck with a tissue and then pressed it against her palms to dry them. She walked to the door and opened it when she heard a firm knocking.

Her eyes grew wide as she recognized the gentleman standing in front of her.

"Oliver Monroe! I can't believe that you're standing here in front of me!" Her head swirled.

"Chloe, you look wonderful. I'm happy to see you again after all these years." He noticed the eternal pain that still held her eyes hostage after losing her family so tragically. He wanted to take her into his arms and make it go away, but instead he held out his hand to shake hers.

She shook his hand with her clammy one remembering the worst day of her entire life. And, how he had given her his highly valued carved box containing the three sand dollars to console her. He was much taller than she last saw him and very handsome with sandy brown hair and a small mustache. Her eyes met his ocean blue ones and her cheeks felt warm as she blushed.

"Come in please and have a seat. I'm quite surprised. I guess I should have read the last name on your application, but all I saw was the name Ollie with your remarkable credentials. I thought that you were going to study family law like your father?"

He smirked embarrassingly. "Ollie is what my patients call me, and its kind off stuck over the years. It was my plan to become a lawyer, but my real interest was optometry so I told my parents the truth. Of course they were disappointed, but it was my happiness that they cared about the most. They have been very supportive. Oh, and Hope, my sister is now a lawyer practicing with my father so everything is good."

"How nice. Doc Benson and I were quite impressed after reading your resume. Would you tell me more about why you chose this practice to become a partner?"

"I love where I work right now, everyone is great and my patients are fantastic. But the commute is killing me. And I would like to be a partner as well as an owner. Regrettably, there is no opportunity for that presently as none of the owners are ready to retire. I've been saving for years for this opportunity and feel that I could do amazing things here. Doc Benson showed me around after our interview, the practice is incredible. Plus, my parents and sister are just down the road so I would be able to spend more time with them." He looked sincere as he spoke.

"I understand. Family is very important." Her face was solemn as she said it and he understood.

"How is your grandmother doing Chloe?" He remembered her as being unbelievably loving and knew she was the light of her life. The last time he seen her was the day of the funeral, which he tried to erase from his mind. The day weighed heavily on his mind for years.

Chloe's eyes lit up as she smiled. "Gran is doing well, thank you for asking. I haven't been able to persuade her to move here with me so I visit her every weekend in Sarnia." Ollie thought that she looked even more beautiful, if that was possible, when she smiled. They chatted more about his resume and the responsibilities associated with the partnership. When they finished, he looked around the office with great fascination.

"Your office is gorgeous. I love the paintings and this desk is spectacular!"

"Thank you, but I can't take any credit for it. My mother decorated it years ago and I never wanted to change a thing. I love it too." Her eyes followed him as he stood up and walked methodically over to the bookcase.

"You kept it? The carved box, you still have it!" He looked incredulously at her as they both remembered that solemn day.

"Yes, it's quite special to me. I always appreciated what you did for me that day and never got to thank you properly. So, thank you for that caring gesture and for giving away a possession that you prized deeply." Her last words caught in her throat and she had to force herself not to bawl her eyes out.

"It was something that I wanted to do. I wish that I could have done more for you." He reached out then and caressed the beloved box before turning back to her. He didn't dare open the lid for he knew that it was bare. The 3 sand dollars were gone forever, buried with her parents and sister he knew. The image burnt in his mind eternally. He thought that she was the bravest person that he had ever met that mournful day.

"I'm glad that you came today. Doc Benson thinks that you're the best candidate for partnership and I feel the same. Would you feel comfortable working with me on a day-to-day basis? I hope that it wouldn't be too awkward?" She looked worried and he shook his head.

Ollie practically soared off the ground with happiness. "No, not at all, I think that we're a perfect fit. This is a business venture and I believe that we both have the same work ethics and compassion for our jobs. But you're not just choosing me because I gave you my treasure box years ago, are you?" He made her smile.

"Never, you truly are the best person for this business and I would be happy to have you as my partner. Business partner, I mean." She was blushing again profusely.

He held out his hand. "Well, then you have a deal partner!" She shook it happily and asked him to come with her to Doc Benson's office. He had just finished seeing his patient and looked up wearily when they both appeared in his doorway and removed his glasses.

He rose quickly when he saw them and went to shake Ollie's hand. "Ollie, it's a pleasure to see you again."

"You as well, Doc." He didn't say anything and waited for Chloe to break the news to him resembling a cat who swallowed the canary.

Chloe was almost bursting when she told him. "Meet the newest partner of Royal Eye Care!"

Doc looked like he was going to cry. "Congratulations Ollie, I couldn't be more pleased. I was extremely worried that we might not be able to find the right fit, but here you are. Welcome!"

"Thank you, Doc., I am excited to begin this next chapter in my life and won't let you down." They promised to be in contact with him over the next period of time. There were mountains of paperwork to be signed as well. Ollie would share Doc Benson's office until he was comfortable with his everyday routine, then Doc would finally retire.

Chloe couldn't slecp that night thinking about Oliver or Ollie. She tossed and turned for hours before finally falling asleep dreaming about him.

Chapter 17

Ollie settled into his role very nicely and all the patients loved his cheery personality and compassionate nature. Glenda raved about him and Chloe felt as though they had won the lottery. She introduced him one day when she was talking to her Gran and she liked him instantly. She bragged that she was an excellent judge of character. His parents and sister came for a tour of the facility the following week and Chloe felt a flooding of memories come back. Ollie's mom was still very lovely with just a touch of gray in her blonde hair. His father quite distinguished looking, but older and Hope had blossomed into a beautiful young woman like her mother.

"Mr. and Mrs. Monroe, what a pleasure to see you again. And you as well Hope!" She hugged them and remembered the enjoyable times that they shared so many years ago. Before her parents and sister passed away, then life had changed drastically for her.

"Please, you must call us Owen and Hannah. It truly is wonderful to see you, Chloe." A shadow cast over her face as she remembered the last time that they all saw each other. The day of the funeral would haunt her forever; her heart ached for Chloe.

"Thank you. And congratulations Hope on becoming a lawyer like your father." She was sincere as she said it.

She blushed and then joked. "I couldn't let him down after my brother did." They all laughed then.

"I'll let Ollie show you around. I'm so happy to have him as a partner." She went back to her office then to allow them time together.

Doc approached her cautiously one day to speak about the upcoming Canadian Association of Optometrists Congress that was fast approaching in July.

"Chloe, would you be terribly disappointed if I didn't accompany you to the CAO Congress as originally planned this year?" He swallowed after he spoke and it sounded more like a gulp.

She smiled to reassure him. "No, not at all. I understand your decision. You're retiring soon so please don't worry."

"Thank you, I appreciate that. I thought that perhaps Ollie could take my place, of course if you feel comfortable with that."

Her heart skipped a beat for some reason. "Yes, I think that's a wonderful idea."

"I haven't spoken to him yet. I wanted to discuss it with you first. I'll go and see if he's free." He looked happy as he left her office with a skip in his step, feeling the weight off his shoulders. It was decided that Ollie would step in for him and Doc would transfer all of the information, including the plane tickets over to him.

On the 6th of June, Doc Benson finally retired with a big farewell party that they all planned for him. It was bittersweet with mixed emotions of happiness and intense feelings of loss. They would all miss him greatly, especially his silly jokes and cheerfulness. Ollie's parents were there as well as his sister. Doc's wife Marie was beaming by his side as she looked forward to spending more time with him and seeing more of the world. Glenda did a wonderful job of hiring a caterer who blew everyone away with an impressive selection of food. All raved about the miniature canapes, lamb lollipops and lobster satays as well as the delectable pastries. The merriment continued as they socialized and enjoyed the abundance of treats. Then, it was time for a toast and the guests held a glass of Champagne in the air as Doc spoke.

"I would like to thank you all for the best first day of my retirement. And although I will enjoy myself immensely travelling and relaxing with my lovely wife, I will also miss all of this and you." He was teary eyed and took a moment to compose before he continued. "Royal Eye Care was always my second home and Glenda and Chloe my second family. And now Ollie, who has made us all very proud. Thank you so much. But all of you must wipe your tears now. Think of the wintertime when Marie and I are in the tropics and you're shovelling mountains of snow.

Cheers!" He laughed then and after raising his glass, took a large sip of the bubbly liquid.

Chloe went to give him a big hug. "I will be forever grateful for you for what you did for me. Take care Doc and keep in touch."

"I will Chloe. Promise me you will not work too hard and enjoy life a little as well." She nodded because her words were stuck in her throat. He hugged Glenda and shook Ollie's hand before walking out the front door happily with his wife. Chloe and Ollie helped tidy up the office after the caterer's left. They had taken care of everything, providing tables and chairs as well as the decorations. And it didn't take long to have it back the way it was beforehand.

"I think that went really well. How strange it will be not seeing him on a daily basis. Sometimes I think the good things always change." Chloe shrugged and looked sad.

"Not true. I'm here and I'm a good thing, aren't I?" Ollie laughed as he blatantly teased her.

She laughed back at him. "Of course you are. A very good thing." They said goodbye to Glenda and strolled outside to a warm, pleasant evening together. Chloe had walked to work that morning like she usually did on the fair-weather days and lifted her face to the sunshine. With her eyes closed, she took a deep breath. She released it slowly and then opened her eyes.

"Can I give you a ride home?" Ollie had parked his car in the private lot around the back of their building.

"No, but thank you. I'll enjoy the fresh air and exercise. Especially after all that gourmet food we had!" Her hand patted her stomach gently.

"Good night, Chloe, enjoy your weekend." She waved goodbye and walked home deep in thought. Thank goodness she had Glenda and Ollie to help her with the practice. Happily, her thoughts changed as she looked forward to visiting her Gran first thing in the morning. There was a fancy new pastry shop that she would stop at beforehand to pick up some pain de chocolate to bring with her.

Chloe woke feeling refreshed and sang as she got ready thinking that she hadn't been this happy in a long while. She had packed her overnight bag the night before and after she drank a cup of tea, she drove to the quaint little shop for the treats. The shelves behind the glass were heaped with the most tantalizing desserts and she couldn't help purchasing some dainty strawberry tarts along with the pain de chocolate. The pleasant owner put the delicacies into pristine white boxes and tied them with a satin ribbon after she put a gold label on top. It was still early so the traffic was light and she relaxed as she drove to Sarnia listening to music. Her Gran was waiting for her on the front porch with Iris and sheer delight radiated from her face as she drove up the laneway. Chloe got out of the car and bent down to pick up Iris in her arms who licked her face happily. She set her down and ran to her Gran to give her a big hug.

"My dear Chloe! I am so happy to see you again."

"Me too. How are you? You look great!" She immediately felt that peace and tranquillity when she was with her. Like a warm blanket on a chilly day.

"Wonderful, especially now that you're here. How was the drive?"

"Very good, no problems at all." She sat down on one of the porch chairs and eagerly accepted a glass of iced tea from her Gran. The glass was decorated with a slice of lemon. After taking a few sips of the perfectly sweetened drink, she went to her car and removed the boxes from the pastry shop back in Oakville.

"What do you have in the boxes Chloe?" Layla was salivating at the thought of something decadent.

"Pain de chocolate and strawberry tartlets. What do you prefer right now?"

"I'd like the pain de chocolate please. Let me get some plates and napkins from the kitchen. I'll be right back. And I'll put the tartlets in the refrigerator. Don't eat without me, not even a nibble." She laughed and then winked at Chloe who giggled back.

"I promise." She undid the pretty satin ribbon and opened the box as her Gran returned.

"How elegant! I bet they're delicious." They chatted as they ate and watched the boats out on the water from her porch. Chloe spoke about Doc Benson's retirement and of her new colleague with a gleam in her eye, which didn't go unnoticed by her Gran.

"Ollie will also be attending the CAO Congress this July with me. I am actually quite looking forward to it." She looked beautiful as she spoke and her Gran felt a long-awaited peace in her heart.

"I know you'll have a marvelous time."

On Sunday after church, they went to the cemetery as customary and replaced the flowers on each of the head stones. They brought big bouquets of tulips in lavender and mauve shades from Layla's gardens. Together they worked to place the lovely arrangements in the flower cups after removing the withered ones. Chloe knew that no matter how many years that passed, she would still feel pain that cut like a knife when she visited them. She thought about her sister and what she would have been doing now if she were alive. Beautiful Ariana. Then, of her mother and how proud she would be today of Chloe following in her footsteps. Blinking hard to stop the welling of tears that brimmed her eyes, she knelt down gingerly to touch the headstone. Her fingers outlined the engraving of her mother's name ***Arabella Burke*** in the marble and stopped abruptly before her father's. It felt cool to the touch, even though it was a warm day. She stood up as though there was a heavy weight burdening her shoulders and joined her Gran who was talking softly to her beloved Winston. Her grandpa's rich marble stone shone against the mid day sun as she gently put her arm around her Gran. Reaching into her handbag, she pulled out two butterscotch candies and gave Chloe one. As they removed the candy from the wrapper, both remembered when she and her sister Ariana placed them on top of his casket. *"Remember savor, don't bite it!"* They were quiet as they enjoyed grandpa's favorite treat, after which leaving to go home arm in arm.

Chloe was all packed for the CAO Congress and waiting for the airline limo to pick her up with Ollie. It was the day of registration and she was most excited to attend the numerous seminars which featured a notable lineup of guest speakers. Glenda was a blessing arranging both of their schedules to accommodate the four-day trip. She also took care of the airline and hotel bookings for which they were most grateful. Her doorbell rang then and after one last look around, she gathered up her luggage and opened the door to a beaming Ollie.

"Hi Ollie! I'm all ready." Her heart did a flip.

A Gran Scheme

"Perfect, let me carry your bags." The driver took the luggage from Ollie as they approached and set them in the trunk.

"I'm really excited to go on this trip. I haven't been anywhere in a very long time." Chloe's face clouded over as she remembered the trips that she used to take with her family. France, Italy and Disneyland, her absolute favorite as a kid.

Ollie smiled at her. "We're going to have a great time. And, I'm going to treat you to the best seafood dinner."

"Sounds good. I can't wait!" They arrived at Pearson International Airport in just under an hour due to some light traffic. Bustling with visitors, the lobby was filled with tourists and they waited in line to use the self-service kiosks. After grabbing a coffee, they sat together until their flight was called. It wasn't long before they were seated comfortably on the plane flight to Halifax, Nova Scotia. The flight didn't seem that long and they were landing before they knew it. Partly because they talked the whole flight, and Chloe hadn't laughed so hard in her entire life. She never imagined that she would have such fun with him. Ollie carried their bags to the car that he had booked to take them to the hotel. It was about a half hour from the airport in the downtown area and neither was disappointed when they arrived.

"Wow, so fancy! I can't wait to check out our rooms." Ollie was practically speechless as he cranked his head around the main lobby. Marble walls with golden chandeliers eluded a warmth and elegance that he wasn't used to.

Chloe was also pleased. "I think I'm going to like staying here!" The concierge escorted each to their rooms pulling the luggage on a trolley. They were adjoining, both with queen-sized beds with a delightful view of the Atlantic Ocean. Glenda did a splendid job with the reservations and both were extremely content. Chloe called her Gran and showed her the room as well as the view.

"The view is captivating. I remember your grandpa and I visited Halifax years ago. We paddled around Peggy's Cove and fell in love with it." She looked wistful as she said it, remembering the special times with her husband. How she missed them dearly.

"It is pretty amazing. I can't wait to see more. And Ollie has been the very best companion so far." Once more, her Gran saw the light in her eyes and a happiness radiate from her that she hadn't seen in a long time. It made her very pleased.

"I'm glad dear. Have the best time and keep in touch."

"I'll call you tomorrow, love you."

"I love you, Chloe. Goodbye." Sighing, she set down her cell phone and went to freshen up.

After freshening up, they went to register and then to attend the opening ceremonies. Later, a scenic cruise was planned on the historic three-masted schooner which traveled along the world's second-largest natural harbor, the Halifax Harbor. Live music enticed them as they observed all of the well-known landmarks of the region.

"This is breathtaking!" Chloe was captivated by the beautiful waterfront sights.

"It is. And look, there's the Northwest Arm!" He was entirely fascinated as she was. They toasted, then he took a drink of his beer as Chloe sipped her wine drinking in not only the beverage, but the view. They sat together and enjoyed a hotdog combo with freshly made popcorn. Ollie laughed as she took a bite and got ketchup on her nose.

"What is so funny?" She hadn't been this joyful in so long.

Ollie took a clean napkin and wiped at her nose. "Ketchup, my dear. More on the tip of your nose than in your mouth most likely."

Blushing, she answered him softly. "Oh, not true. But thank you anyways!" Her hazel eyes glowed and often, the wind picked up a tendril of her chestnut hair framing her delicate face. She wore a white off the shoulder blouse with jeans and he thought that she looked gorgeous. His heart did a somersault as he swallowed, then looked away.

"Tomorrow night, I would like to treat you to a real dinner at a seafood restaurant not far from our hotel. Unless, of course you'd rather have hotdogs again?" He smiled wryly at her.

"Not really! I'd love that." She couldn't help but to linger on his face longer that she wanted. He made her feel as though she was in a dream, lightheaded and whimsical. As the sun began to set, the boat began to make its way back to the harbour and Chloe wished that the moment would last forever.

The next morning both were up early to attend the first session on Eyes on Oncology which both found interesting and then one specific to dry eyes. There was a lunch break in between and Chloe couldn't wait for her dinner date with Ollie later. *Date? Dare she call it that?* It excited her to think about it and she was completely lost in thought while the lecturer spoke candidly about Scleral Lens. She practically jumped for joy when they returned to the hotel to dress for dinner. She had brought two stylish dresses and after careful consideration, she chose the red halter one. She showered beforehand and dried her hair before putting in soft curls with the iron. Taking a black liner, she made up her eyes and then selected a bright red lipstick the exact shade of the dress. As she ran the shiny lipstick over her perfectly shaped lips, her mind was filled with magical thoughts of Ollie. Blushing a shade that was almost as red as her lipstick, she stood up quickly to dress. Lastly, she misted some perfume. He tapped on her door just moments later and she opened it to find him outfitted in a pair of dress pants with a shirt and tie.

Ollie gasped when he saw her. "Wow, you look incredible. You are so beautiful." He was raving, but he couldn't stop himself.

"Thank you. You look very nice also." He took her arm as they rode the elevator down to the lobby and outside.

"Are you fine to walk a few minutes?" She was wearing dressy shoes and he didn't want to inconvenience her.

"Yes, these have a wedge heel and are super comfortable." She was touched that he was worried about her comfort. The restaurant was literally just steps away and they were greeted warmly by the host who immediately sat them. The table was one of the best in the house, located by the window with a gorgeous view of the harbourfront. They began by ordering a bottle of Sauvignon Blanc which delighted their palate with a light and fruity burst of pleasure. The candlelight enhanced the experience and made it very romantic as they read the menus.

"What do you think about us each ordering the seafood platter?" Ollie couldn't stop looking at her, she was captivating.

A Gran Scheme

She read the dish out loud as her eyes grew wide. "Goodness. Scallops, jumbo shrimp, halibut, clams and a lobster tail with risotto! I think I just died and went to heaven."

He laughed at her. "Done, it's decided then. We might not be able to eat for a couple of days after, but it will be definitely worth the price." They put in the order which pleased the server and even began with an order of the crabcakes which were Ollie's favorite.

"Thank you for making this such a memorable time. I never expected this trip to be such a pleasurable one." The intense pain of her past still showed itself every once in a while, and he admired her courage.

"I should be thanking you. For the opportunity you gave me. And for the joy that I feel not only working with you, but spending time with you." He looked sincere as he said it to her and she suddenly felt shy. He reached for her hand then and held it gently as tears filled their eyes. It was silent, but both knew how much she missed her family.

"We have the crab cakes here for you!" The server set them down in the middle of the table as they reluctantly let go of each others hand.

"Mm... these look delicious." The tasted as good as they looked and they finished them while their glasses were filled with wine.

"Did you know that this restaurant was once home to the oldest mortuary for victims of the Titanic tragedy in 1912? Oh, and again in 1917 after the Halifax explosion."

Chloe looked shocked. "Really? How morbid and sad." She looked around then taking in the heritage building and its extensive renovations.

He told her more. "Almost 2,000 lives were lost when a French munitions ship struck another vessel in the harbor. Originally, this building was a school before it was purchased by the Snow family who used it as a funeral home."

"That is fascinating. No one would ever guess that now by looking around. The décor was comfortable and pleasing.

"I totally agree. They say that this place is haunted. That cutlery falls off tables and glasses drop off the shelves for no reason at all. Gray, fog like patches move slowly through the buildings and many people have saw them."

Chloe's eyes grew wide as he chuckled. "You're really enjoying this aren't you?" Just then, an explosion of shattering glass behind the bar caused him to jump in his seat and she couldn't help but snicker. "A ghost perhaps?"

His face was as red as the lobster that they served there. "Very funny! It is quite interesting though." The seafood feast came and it did not disappoint. Fit for a king and queen, they were satiated by the time they finished most of it.

"I think that we polished it off well, don't you think?" Ollie was practically groaning as he said it.

"Oh, yes. I probably won't be able to walk out of here now though." Chloe massaged her stomach and giggled.

"I'll carry you back to the hotel then."

"What a sight that will be! Let's take a walk and explore the area."

He paid the bill and they strolled down Argyle Street taking in the numerous restaurants, pubs and patios which overflowed onto the streets. It was a lively atmosphere and Chloe wanted the evening to last forever. Ollie's hand ached to take hers, but he was worried that she might think that he was acting too fast. The feelings that he was developing for her were becoming more difficult to keep inside and he could only pray that she felt the same way. Back at the hotel, they reluctantly said goodnight to each other.

"Thank you so much for the lovely evening, Ollie. I enjoyed myself and the food was fabulous." Her lips looked full and inviting and he was quiet, mesmerized by her beauty. "Are you okay?"

He spoke, perhaps too quickly. "Yes, of course! I loved it as well. See you in the morning Chloe, sleep tight." His lips burned for hers as he walked to his room. He dreamed of his sweet angel, feeling intoxicated by her until he woke.

Over the next few days, their time was filled with not only the congress speakers, but an abundance of sightseeing. They explored the 4-kilometer-long waterfront stopping to discover the shops then delighting in a lobster roll with fresh cut fries and ice-cold beer. The Atlantic Ocean breeze was refreshing as they observed people strolling past while enjoying on the patio. On a whim, they went into an art gallery and at the LONDONDERRY Market,

A Gran Scheme

Chloe found a stunning blouse for her Gran. Elegant, like her, Chloe knew that she would love it. On the last night of the CAO, both attended the closing dinner which presented gourmet food highlighting delicacies from the area. Musical entertainers performed while they danced together. Ollie held her close for a romantic song and she fell hopelessly in love with him then.

Their visit to Halifax ended with a tour of Georges Island National Historic Site and then Peggy's Cove. Travelling on foot, they explored the village. The lighthouse which sat at the entrance to St. Margaret's Bay, built in 1915 and rested upon huge boulders enthralled them. Ollie was especially touched by the Monument to Nova Scotia fisherman. The sculpture was carved into a wall of rock depicting 32 fisherman and their families.

Chapter 18

Chloe settled back in with Ollie at their optometry practice, both still raving about their visit to Halifax. As she was leaving Wednesday evening, Ollie caught her off guard by asking her to go to dinner and bowling on Friday night with his sister and her boyfriend. Fridays were shorter days at the optometry office.

"Unless you don't like bowling, then we could plan for something else." He looked like a kid as he waited for her to answer.

"I'd love that, Ollie. I used to go bowling with my family every weekend, but that was years ago." Whenever she spoke about them, his heart ached for her. Relieved that she said yes, he began to breathe again. "Fantastic, I'll pick you up at 6:00 if that's good with you."

"Perfect, see you Friday night then." Chloe practically floated home like she was on a cloud. After calling her Gran, she relaxed with a light dinner on her balcony and read a book. After only a few pages, she caught herself thinking of him again. Ollie made her heart sing; he was very special. But she couldn't allow herself to think about him that way. And falling in love with him was not an option. They were partners and co-workers so she had to remove the romantic thoughts that were unleashing in her mind.

Chloe practically flew out of the office early Friday afternoon, overjoyed for her upcoming date with Ollie. No, not a date, she reminded herself!

"You're in a hurry, Chloe." Glenda had stayed later to finish up some business and was also getting ready to leave.

Chloe blushed profusely. "Oh, just excited to start the weekend. Any plans for you and the grandchildren?"

"It's been so hot, that we're going to go to the waterpark and have a picnic. The kids should have a blast and love the many waterslides that they have there." The look in her eye told Chloe that she was suspicious about her behaviour.

"Wow, they will enjoy that. Have fun Glenda and see you on Monday." Excited, she took a long walk along the waterfront, then returned home to dig for treasure in her closet. Since it was a casual date, she finally decided on bell bottom jeans and a pink lacy camisole top. Chloe was dressed and ready almost an hour before. Every time she walked by a mirror, she stared at herself in it, scrutinizing the outfit and her makeup. Finally, she just stopped walking by the mirrors and began to relax. The doorbell rang shortly afterwards. Ollie was always on time and she loved that.

"Hi Ollie, I'm all ready!" She sounded breathless.

"Great. Hope and her boyfriend Brody are going to meet us at the restaurant. I love your outfit." His eyes didn't miss the curve of the jeans over her body or the thin lacy top that she wore.

She smiled. "Thanks!" They were already waiting for them at the table when they arrived. The ladies ordered a bottle of red wine and the men draught beer. He had chosen a steak house that people raved about and they each chose filet mignon as their main course. Chloe loved talking to Hope, she was down to earth and very sweet. Her boyfriend also extremely pleasant and funny. The conversation was casual and light, full of laughter and Ollie teased everyone that he would beat them at bowling.

Chloe pouted. "I hope that bowling is just like riding a bicycle. Once you learn, you never forget."

"I think that it's more like golf, it requires practice to keep up performance." He grinned at her with his perfectly white teeth.

Hope chimed in. "My bet is on Chloe." She toasted her then laughing.

"We'll see!" The bowling alley was busy and he was glad that he reserved a lane for them. It was five pin, he preferred that and so did the others.

"You're up first, good luck!" He was smug Chloe thought as she picked up a green marbled ball and held it in front of her. After taking a few very precise steps, she brought her hand back smoothly and released the ball onto the laneway knocking down all five pins.

"Great shot Chloe!" She could tell that he thought that it was beginners' luck as he clapped loud and cheered for her. On his turn, he left two pins standing. In the end, Chloe had three strikes and Ollie just one. Brody did well and Hope struggled a bit but had a great time. It was so much fun, but she felt that the evening had gone by too fast.

On Monday when she returned to her office, there was a small white bag on her desk and with great curiosity she walked over to it. Her breath caught as she unwrapped three perfect sand dollars. Bleached white from the sun, she lifted one and felt its smooth hard shell. Then, she held it to close to her heart as she cried for the family that she lost so many years ago. Her body wrenching with pain, she missed them so much. Solemnly, she carried them to the wooden box on the shelf that Ollie had given her during the most horrific time of her life. They were reminiscence of the day she placed them on top of her mother's, father's and sister's caskets. All three snatched greedily from her life and she had been angry with God for years. Hypnotized, she lifted the lid before tenderly placing them inside to rest.

Ollie made her a promise a long time ago that one day she would fill it again with more sand dollars. He made sure of it. Chloe closed the lid and went back to sit at her desk for a moment to gather her thoughts. She opened her locket, feeling the warmth from her mother's smile in the first photograph. For years, she had mixed emotions when she looked at her father's, blaming him for the tragedy. Now, she just felt sorrow. Her breath caught when she looked at her sister Ariana, forever immortalized as a beautiful young woman.

A gentle knock on the office door brought her back to the present and she closed the locket quickly. Grabbing tissue, she blew her nose and blotted her eyes before going to answer it.

Ollie noticed her puffy eyes and felt regret. "I didn't mean to cause you more pain Chloe, I'm so sorry."

"No, thank you for the sand dollars, Ollie, it was a very touching thing to do."

"I found these ones in Turks and Caicos years ago and prayed that one day I would be able to give them to you. So, the box wouldn't be empty."

"How beautiful. They mean so much." She had a feeling of fullness in her heart.

He wanted to take her in his arms and kiss her pain away. "I'm glad, you're a special woman Chloe." He left her then, frightened that he might say more, reveal his true feelings.

They continued with their weekly dinners and outings throughout the whole summer. In early October, she invited him to Thanksgiving at her Gran's house in Sarnia. She told him that she usually stayed for the weekend when she went, hoping that wouldn't scare him from joining her.

He was touched. "I would like that very much Chloe. Can I bring anything?"

"Just yourself. We put on quite a spread. Turkey, stuffing, mashed potatoes and vegetables. And desert, don't let me forget that. Pies, apple and pumpkin. So delicious." She was already dreaming about sharing the occasion with him.

"I make a mean stuffing; my mother showed me how. Maybe I can make that for you." He looked eager to help.

"Sounds so good. Okay, you're in charge of the stuffing." They worked out the fine details and the thought of spending the weekend with him made her giddy.

The weather had turned cooler quickly and many trees were flaunting their bright fall colors as they drove to Sarnia. They admired the scenery and chatted nonstop the entire way. Chloe was excited for her Gran to meet Ollie in person. She had only spoke to him several times via facetime. Ollie had brought a lovely floral arrangement for the table and reached for it after he helped Chloe out of the car.

Layla opened the door immediately for them as they made their way up the steps. "Happy Thanksgiving you two!" She gave them each a big hug.

"Happy Thanksgiving Gran. It's so good to be here. I'd like you to formally meet Ollie. Ollie, this is my wonderful Gran." Chloe was beaming.

"It's very nice to finally meet you." Ollie felt very much at ease with her. She was truly special and he fully understood the bond they shared.

Layla thought him sincere and liked him right away. "You as well. How pleasant to have you here. Welcome." Chloe hung up her coat and chatted with her Gran while Ollie went to the car to get their overnight bags. They went upstairs where she showed him his room and then where to set her bags. They joined Layla back in the kitchen where she was baking up a storm and the different aromas were tantalizing Chloe's tastebuds.

"What can we do to help Gran? Ollie says that he makes the best stuffing."

"Lovely, I'll take him up on that. Hopefully, we have all of the ingredients that you need Ollie."

"I'll make due, don't worry. This is an old family recipe that I think everyone will love." He began immediately after Layla showed him where everything was in the kitchen.

"Chloe, will you make the apple pie for us?" The pumpkin pie was finished and cooling on the baking rack.

"Yes, I would enjoy that." The day went by in a blink of an eye and tired from all of the thanksgiving preparations, they walked down to the main street to have fish and chips for dinner.

Alana was busy wiping tables and ran over to see them. "What a pleasant surprise! Happy Thanksgiving weekend." She was eyeing Ollie with great fascination.

"Happy Thanksgiving to you and your family. I would like you to meet Ollie, my business associate. Ollie, this is Alana the owner."

"Nice to meet you, Ollie." She shook his hand and winked at Chloe who blushed a beet red shade.

"I hear that you have the best fries in all of the country! Not to mention the fish." His mouth was watering as he said it.

Alana laughed. "Yes, it's true! Maybe the world even. My daughter Chanel is off this afternoon so let me put in the order for you." When they were finished eating, Ollie spoke.

"Now I know where to get the very best fish and chips in the whole world!"

Chloe nodded. "I told you so."

Layla's neighbors Lena, Taylor and the children would be joining them in the afternoon on Sunday for dinner after their church service. They had become like second family to her. Caring and compassionate, Chloe was extremely thankful to have them in her Gran's life. Especially after what June and Carl did to them. Thinking of it sent shivers down her spine.

Chloe and her Gran dressed for church while Ollie prepared eggs benedict for them in the kitchen. They were greeted warmly with tea and coffee as they entered. He then expertly whisked the hollandaise sauce while speaking to them.

"Good morning. How did you both sleep?" He was looking dapper in a dress shirt and tie.

"Wonderful. How about you Ollie? Was the bed comfortable?" Layla had been meaning to change out the bed in the guestroom for ages and hoped that he wasn't inconvenienced. She hadn't got around to ordering another mattress for the second room either. Only Chloe's had a new one after the ordeal with June and Carl.

"Best sleep ever actually. The mattress was like sleeping on a cloud." He looked as though he meant it as he served them the extravagant meal.

Chloe was impressed. Smart, good looking, compassionate and a chef. "Gosh, this looks spectacular! Thank you, Ollie."

"My absolute pleasure." He sat down with them to savor the hearty breakfast. Afterwards, they stuffed the turkey and put it into the oven to bake slowly for most of the day. Ollie accompanied them to the cemetery when the service was done and it hit him like a bolt of lightening when he saw the mass headstones. His mind went back to that pitiful day as a young boy remembering the grief. He stayed back to allow them to visit feeling mournful for their immense losses. Chloe smiled when her Gran offered him a butterscotch candy and he stood there with them deep in thought. Their agony tugging at his heart.

The succulent aroma of turkey reached them as soon as they opened the door.

"Yum! Smells heavenly in here." Chloe couldn't wait to relish the cornucopia of food that they all would enjoy later. Layla made up the assorted appetizers on fancy serving dishes as Ollie helped Chloe with setting the table. She remembered the dining room where they used to eat before it became her Gran's bedroom. Now it was quaint having it in the kitchen. Chloe admired the harvest China as she set each plate down on the place setting and Ollie set the silverware. There were matching candles as well as an array of mini white and orange pumpkins. Bronze ceramic turkeys stood nestled with them. The flowers complimented it all with vivacious shades of orange, rust and cream.

"This looks amazing! You guys really do go all out." He felt like kissing her, he was so happy.

She felt guilty for a moment. "Thank you. Yes, my Gran loves this time of year and Christmas. I hope that your family was okay with you coming here instead."

"Of course. I'll catch up with them next week. And sometimes they even go away somewhere warm so mother doesn't have to cook." He was half joking and Chloe laughed. Layla's neighbors arrived just as the appetizers were being set out and the children gleefully ran to sample them.

"Bide your manners please, Jade and Miles!" Lena was clucking at them like a mother hen as they ladened their plates with cheese, crackers and fruit. Layla was in her glory.

After they enjoyed the delightful feast and the dishes were done, Ollie and Chloe slipped out for a walk along the waterfront. The sun was already setting as they observed the view while the wind nipped hungrily at their faces. Fortunately, both wore heavier coats and Chloe had put up her hood to keep warm. Blissfully, they held hands as they walked down the lit pathway to the lighthouse and then casually back, deep in conversation. They chose a park bench beside the Bluewater bridges and sat down contentedly staring out onto the water. Each of the light posts mirrored their reflection in the lake.

"Chloe, these past months have been the best ever in my whole life. I don't want to scare you, but I have fallen deeply in love with you." He felt as though he could faint and had to force himself to take deep breaths. What if she didn't feel the same way?

Chloe's dreams had finally come true. "I love you so much, Ollie!" He took her into his arms and kissed her sending a shockwave throughout her whole body. Then he got up and did a funny dance.

"You do? I feel like screaming that from the top of the bridge!"

Chloe giggled lightheadedly. "No one will hear you. And you might be arrested!"

"I am so happy Chloe. I wish that I would have told you months ago how I felt."

"Well, you know what they say. Hindsight is 20/20!"

Ollie laughed. "I see that you have an "eye" for humor." They kissed again and walked back to her Gran's house holding onto hands tightly.

It was a chilly Friday night in November, when Ollie invited Chloe over for Chinese food dinner at his place. He picked her up at her home and brought her back to enjoy it with him. The table was set beautifully with a soft glow eliminating from the candlelight and fresh flowers carefully arranged in a glass vase.

"Wow, this is fancy!" Chloe sat down when he pulled the chair out for her and accepted a glass of wine. "Thank you." He poured himself a glass and toasted her as they both took a sip. His lips met her then and they were both breathless afterwards.

Ollie then removed each container from the bag and served the various dishes on her plate. "I hope you like it madame. Bon appetite! Because I don't know how to say it in Chinese."

"I will. It looks fabulous." He used chopsticks, she a fork and knife. They devoured almost everything and afterwards he invited her to sit in front of the fireplace with him. It was warm and cozy, and Chloe was feeling very relaxed sprawled out beside him.

Ollie handed her a fortune cookie and took one for himself. Cracking it open, he read his fortune out loud to her.

"You have met the woman of your dreams." His eyes met hers as she giggled and blushed profusely.

"Let me see what mine says." She snapped the cookie in half, popping a piece in her mouth. "A marriage proposal is in the near future." She gasped as he got up from the rug on one knee and holding a ring spoke to her.

"I can't believe my good "fortune" in finding you again. It has been the greatest joy to be your partner in business. And it would be my dream come true for you to be my partner in life as well. To roll through the "sweet and sour" times. Maybe have some little "dumplings" of our own. I've been "wonton" to ask you to marry me for so long now. I love you Chloe Burke, will you be my wife?" Tears flooded his eyes as he waited for her to respond.

"Yes, I will marry you! Your "wok" my world Ollie. I would love to be your wife. It was incredibly cheesy, but she adored it. She was crying with happiness as he put the ring on her finger and kissed her longingly. She gasped when she held up her hand.

"Oh, my goodness! This exquisite ring, it was passed down many generations to Anna and my Gran inherited it." Tearfully, she recalled how her mother's dear friend and neighbor was stricken with cancer and passed away. Without every knowing that her son Felix had predeceased her. The malevolent actions of June and Carl had cost them much grief and she was glad to know that they would be locked up for a very long time.

Ollie replied lovingly. "Yes, I asked your Gran for your hand in marriage at Thanksgiving and she was thrilled. She asked me to stay put. When she returned, she carried the small box. I opened it and was astonished because she wanted me to give it you when I proposed. She told me the touching story behind it. I kept it safe ever since planning for this day." His parents and sister Hope were thrilled when he told them he was proposing.

"I am at a lost for words. This is more than I could ever have dreamed of. I am so thrilled." The evening was enchanted and she couldn't wait thank her Gran for the special keepsake.

Chloe and Ollie stopped at her favorite French bakery to purchase a cake before driving down to visit her Gran for the weekend. The owner Eloise beamed when she walked in with Ollie and greeted them warmly.

"Bonjour, it's good to see you again. What indulgences are you here for today?"

"We would like a celebration cake, something breathtaking and very elegant." Chloe held up her hand in glee and felt as though she was about to burst with happiness.

Eloise squealed in delight. "Félicitations, how wonderful! "She showed them several cakes before they decided on a small raspberry buttercream one. "Ahh, a very good choice. Inside is a delightful lemon curd filling. Also, perfect for a wedding cake." She winked at them as she wrapped it up in the trademark box tied prettily with a ribbon, then the gold sticker. She also gave them a box of croissants complimentary to enjoy with butter and strawberry preserves. This time, even with the excellent conversation and company, the drive to Sarnia seemed to be taking forever. It was also starting to snow lightly, and Ollie turned on the wipers to clear it from the windshield.

"How much longer? I wish we were there." Chloe was squirming in her seat and fiddling with her phone.

"That's because you can't wait to show your Gran that pretty ring on your finger. Another half an hour to go, my darling." He took her hand and kissed it, feeling proud to be engaged to her. They arrived in Sarnia to a postcard greeting of snow-covered trees, but Chloe didn't even notice the beauty.

"Finally!" Chloe practically leapt out of the car before it stopped and ran up the steps

A Gran Scheme

to see her Gran. Ollie carried the boxes from the bakery as snowflakes danced against the gray sky backdrop. The door opened and they were welcomed in with sheer pleasure.

"Hello! Congratulations on your engagement!" Layla shone in a mauve blouse and navy pants with her smooth white hair clipped back as she gave them both an enormous hug. Chloe thought that she had never looked happier and felt the same.

Chloe held out her hand to show the ring. "Thank you, Gran, I am touched by your generous gift. It is something that I will always treat as sacred and meaningful. I adore you." Her Gran's arms made her feel such warmth and love.

"Hey, can we make this a group hug?" He was grinning like a youngster as he held out his arms.

Gran spied the boxes on the hall table. "Did you bring goodies for us to enjoy?"

"Sure did! Would you like to have it now?" Ollie knew that he didn't even have to ask.

"Yes!" Both she and Chloe answered at once and led the way to the kitchen. Chloe was already removing plates from the cupboard while her Gran rubbed her hands in delight as she made a pot of tea. Ollie untied the signature ribbon and opened the box to reveal the delicate cake.

Gran clapped. "This is just perfect for the occasion! Tell me about the proposal." Ollie served the cake as Chloe explained how he asked her to marry him over a romantic Chinese food dinner. Tinkled pink, her Gran chuckled. Then Chloe spoke about their plans for a wedding in the upcoming spring.

Layla thought about Chloe's birthday which was also in the spring. "Such a delightful time of the year for a wedding. Everything is reawakening and starting fresh. I have always been fond of the springtime." Her face held a calmness as she spoke. "My, this cake is scrumptious."

"Gran, could we have the wedding here? In the backyard by the gazebo?" Chloe popped a forkful of the moist cake into her mouth and closed her eyes as she savored it.

"Wonderful idea, Chloe. My tulips in shades of mauve, violet and lavender will be in full bloom." Her eyes held excitement. She thought that the elegant white structure with the pillars would be a beautiful backdrop for the affair.

Chloe marvelled at the thought of tulips. "Yes, that sounds perfect! I would love to plan the wedding around those colors as well." Ollie sat quietly in all his glory drinking his tea and relishing in the thought of being married to his one true love. And Chloe felt as though her heart was finally healing.

"I do believe also, that the guests should shower you with rice after the ceremony. It would be most fitting, don't you agree?" Layla was trying to keep a straight face.

Looking just as serious, Ollie answered. "Yes, just as long as it's not fried rice!" They all laughed, feeling great contentment. The joy that Chloe and her Gran so yearned for had finally come to bless them.

Manufactured by Amazon.ca
Bolton, ON